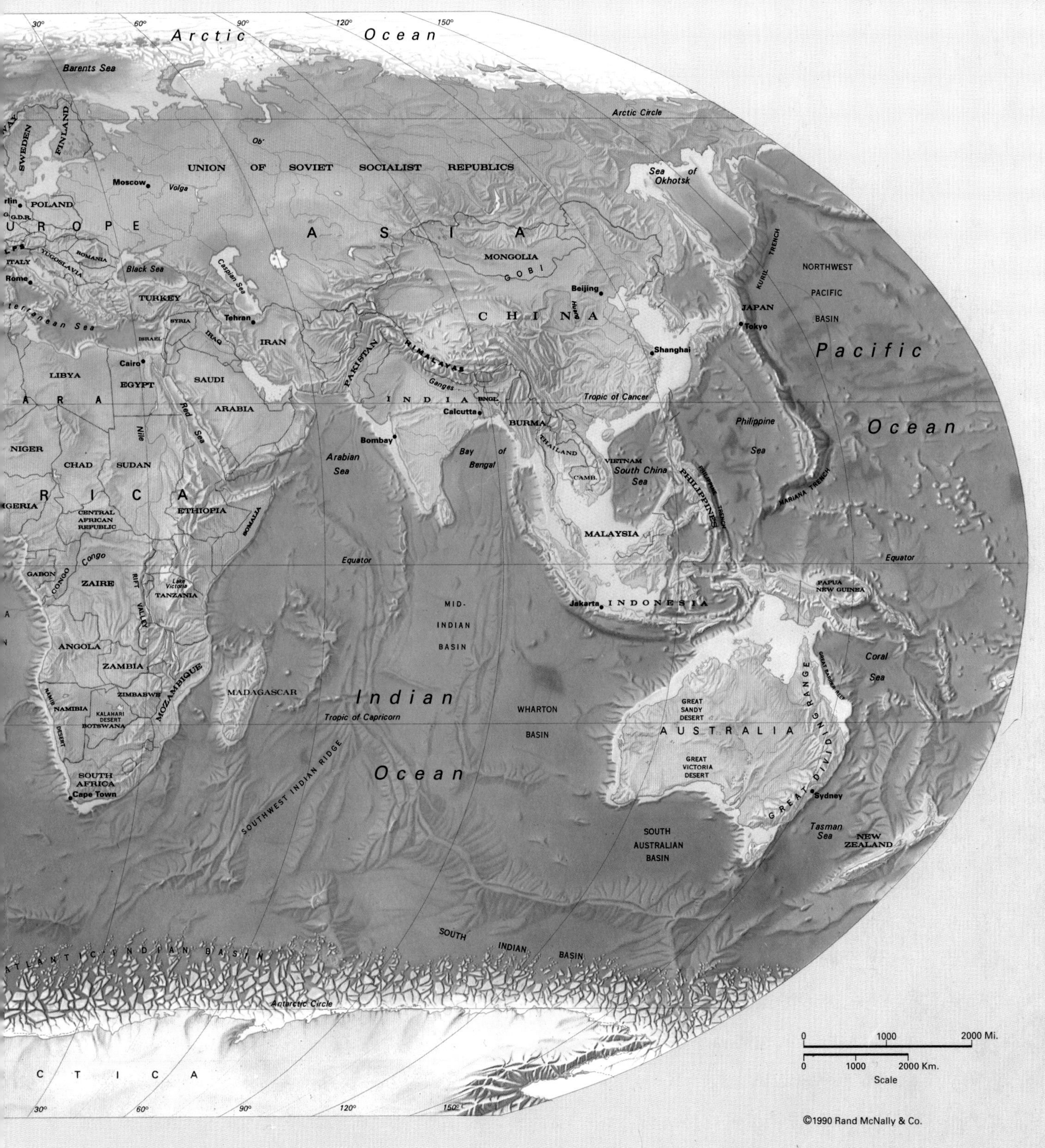

0 1000 2000 Mi.
0 1000 2000 Km.
Scale

Rand McNally

Children's Atlas of Earth through Time

Rand McNally
Chicago • New York • San Francisco

Rand McNally Children's Atlas of Earth through Time

General manager: Russell L. Voisin
Managing editor: Jon M. Leverenz
Editor: Elizabeth G. Fagan
Writer: Francis Reddy
Designer: Corasue Nicholas
Illustrators: Jan Wills, Pat Ortega
Production editor: Laura C. Schmidt
Production manager: Patricia Martin

Published in the United States of America. Printed in Italy.

Photograph credits
8-9: Coral reef and rain forest/United States Geological Service. 13: Galaxy/© J.D. Wray. 22-23: Grand Canyon/United States Geological Service. Fossils/Dinosaur National Monument/National Park Service. 24-25: Dinosaur fossils/Dinosaur National Monument/National Park Service. Robber fly fossil/Florissant Fossil Beds National Monument. Fish fossil/Florissant Fossil Beds National Monument. 34-35: Silurian reef/Milwaukee Public Museum. 36-37: Coelacanth/©Professor Hans Fricke/Max Planck Institut für Verhaltersphysiologie. 38-39: Shrub fossil/Florissant Fossil Beds National Monument. 40-41: Appalachians/NASA. 44-45: Fossils/Dinosaur National Monument/National Park Service. 66-67: Skulls/Institute of Human Origins. 68-69: Olduvai Gorge/Stephen J. Kraseman/AllStock. 70-71: Sunrise over Chicago/Archie Lieberman. 72-73: Earthrise/NASA.

Library of Congress Catalog Card Number: 90-53225
ISBN: 0-528-83415-0

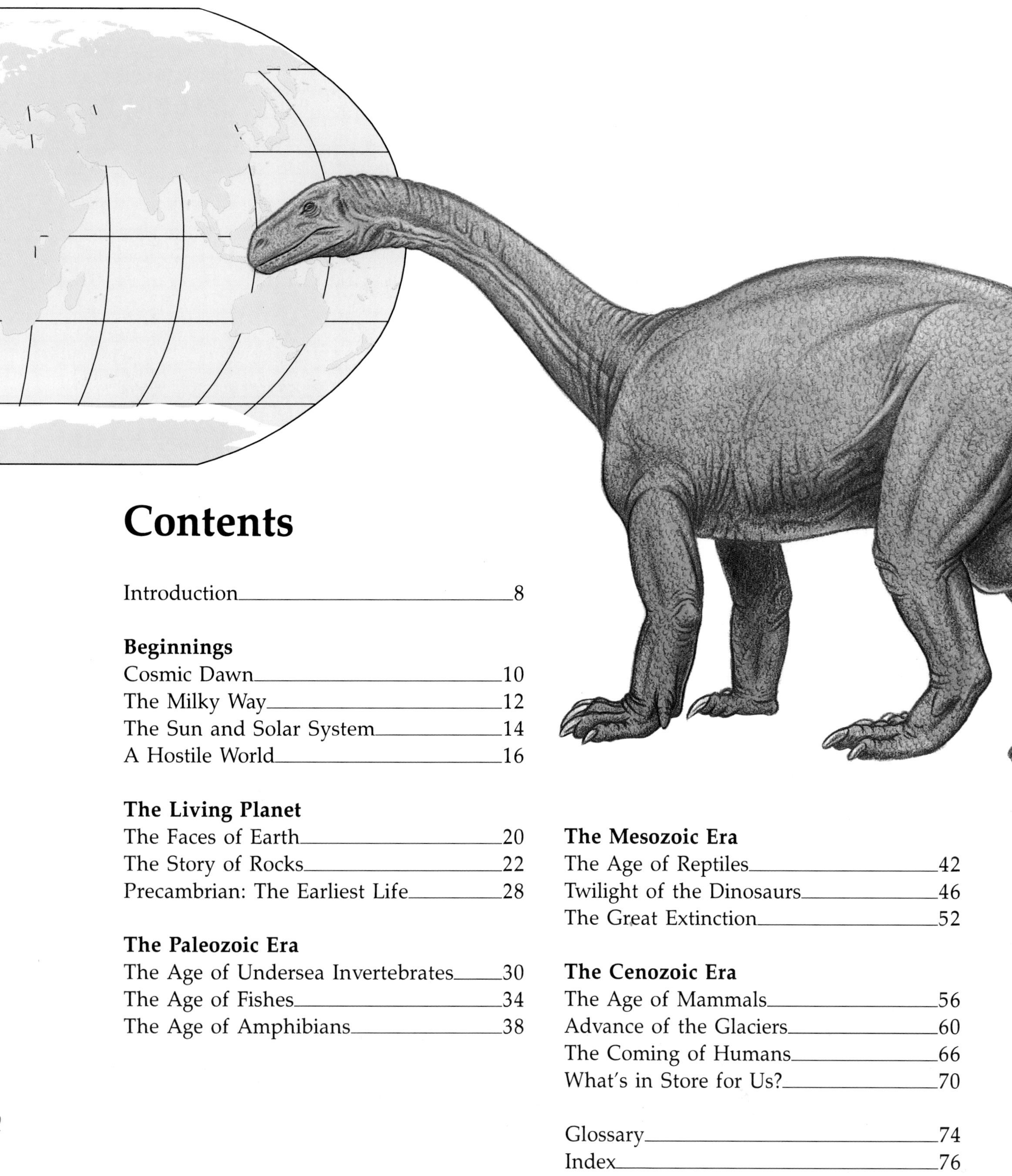

Contents

Galaxies and stars existed for billions of years before planet Earth formed. Life, from a tropical rain forest (far left) to a coral reef, is Earth's unique feature.

Introduction

Only in the twentieth century have people begun to appreciate how truly ancient the world is. About two hundred years ago, experts claimed that the planet was just six thousand years old. As scientists learned more about how rocks form and wear away, they realized that Earth was far older than this. Yet even in the last years of the nineteenth century, most scientists counted the Earth's age in millions of years. Estimates by even the boldest scientists of the day approached less than 10 percent of Earth's true age.

Today, most scientists agree that the Earth and other planets in the solar system formed about 4.5 billion years ago. Evidence comes from the Earth, the Moon, and from space debris called meteorites. To grasp this enormous length of time, imagine that the width of a single human hair represents one year. A human life span would occupy a pencil's width; the history of civilization would fall within the distance covered by a single footstep. A thirty-minute drive on a highway would span the fossil record, but Earth's long history would continue on for another 250 miles (402 kilometers). Extending this hair's breadth scale to the beginning of the universe would add more than 1,100 miles (1,800 kilometers) to it.

This book is a step-by-step journey through time. Think of it as a movie, with each scene providing a glimpse into some part of the deep past. The story begins with the Big Bang, the explosive birth of the universe, and continues through the eons as galaxies, stars, and the solar system are created. The most wonderful part of the story comes last. It is the miraculous parade of creatures that have lived on Earth's surface through the ages. It is the story of life.

BEGINNINGS

Cosmic Dawn

Some eighteen billion years ago, time, space, and energy burst forth in a tremendous explosion. Scientists have nicknamed the event the "Big Bang." They can describe the universe throughout all but the first few fractions of a second after its birth. The cosmos was so hot and dense during the birth of the universe that all the known laws of science completely break down.

Everything in the universe began as part of an expanding fireball of unimaginable heat. The brilliant ball expanded very quickly and started to cool. Before the universe was even four minutes old, the particles that make up the nucleus of an atom had appeared. Hydrogen and helium, the first chemical elements, were born. By the end of its first hour, the universe had cooled and thinned out too much to continue making chemical elements.

Time began with a bang—the Big Bang, a vast fireball that created the cosmos. Hydrogen and helium formed in the first few minutes, but stable atoms and molecules could not appear for a million years.

Yet at the end of the first year, the cosmos was still as hot as the center of a star. It would take another million years before the first stable atoms could form, and over a billion years before galaxies would begin to appear.

The universe is still expanding today. Galaxies are racing away from one another at tremendous speed, riding the continual expansion of space. Using special telescopes sensitive to radio waves, astronomers have detected the echo of the Big Bang. This discovery, in 1965, ranks as one of astronomy's most important. The echo is a faint background of radio noise emitted from every part of the sky. It is a fossil from the earliest days of the cosmos. It is the brilliant glow from the era when those first atoms formed, stretched out by cosmic expansion into a whispering hiss of radio waves.

The Milky Way

About a million years after the Big Bang, the universe was a hot sea of hydrogen and helium gas. As the universe expanded, tiny irregularities in its makeup grew. Over the next billion years, these lumps of gas grew into vast, swirling clouds called *protogalaxies.* One of these clouds eventually became the Milky Way galaxy.

Slowly, the cloud began to collapse. Gravity pulled it into a tighter ball, compressing it and forcing it to spin ever faster. It flattened into a thin disk of gas. Small knots of gas formed within this swirling disk, and they too contracted. The knots grew denser and hotter as they shrank, eventually reaching the point where they produced energy by turning hydrogen into helium. These were the first stars.

The first generation of stars burned brightly and fiercely during their brief careers. Their furnaces forged the heavy chemical elements that had not been created when the universe was born. The new elements included carbon, oxygen, silicon, and iron. Many of these first stars exploded, scattering the new

The spiral galaxy known as NGC 891 shows how the Milky Way would appear if seen on its edge. Its light has taken forty-three million years to reach Earth.

New stars illuminated the Milky Way galaxy in its final stage of formation, about twelve billion years ago.

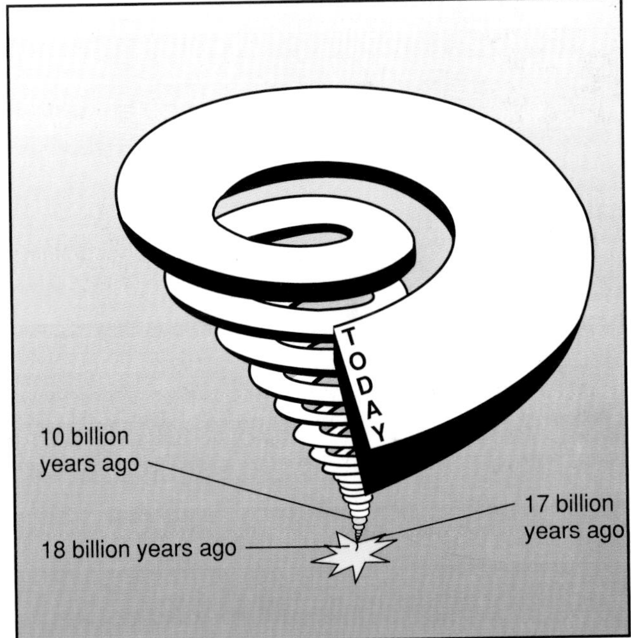

The galaxies were formed between seventeen billion and ten billion years ago.

elements throughout the young Milky Way.

In the galaxy's outer regions, hundreds of thousands of stars formed into tight clusters. Called *globular clusters,* these star balls orbit the flattened disk of the Milky Way and contain the oldest stars visible today.

In the Milky Way's disk, new stars formed within dark dusty clouds filled with the new heavy elements. As hot, bright stars burned their way out of the clouds that created them, they outlined the unwinding spiral arms of the Milky Way galaxy.

The Sun and Solar System

Within the turbulent darkness of a giant dust cloud, a small pocket of gas and dust started to collapse about 4.6 billion years ago. Just why the cloud began to contract no one knows. Many believe the blast wave of a nearby exploding star compressed the cloud and led to the creation of the Sun.

Once started, the cloud's contraction sustained itself and it grew smaller and denser. It rotated faster and faster as it collapsed, and the increased spin flattened the cloud into a disk of gas and dust. Deep within the center of the inward-falling cloud, the compressed gas became further squeezed. Then, just a few million years after the collapse had started, the temperature and density reached a critical point. Hydrogen nuclei slammed together to form helium nuclei, releasing energy. The Sun was born.

By the time the Sun had ignited its inner fires, the planets already had started to form. Tiny dust grains had collided and stuck together, forming sand grains, pebbles, boulders, and larger bodies. Eventually these bodies grew large enough for their gravity to attract other material to them. These *protoplanets* were built up by the gradual sweeping up of other matter.

The conditions within the collapsing cloud help explain why planets near the Sun are rocky and why those far from the Sun are made mostly of gas. Near the forming Sun, high temperatures kept substances like water, methane, and ammonia from condensing into solids. From Mercury out to beyond Mars, the protoplanets formed from rock and metal. Farther out, where cooler temperatures let water and other gases freeze, the solar system's giant planets formed.

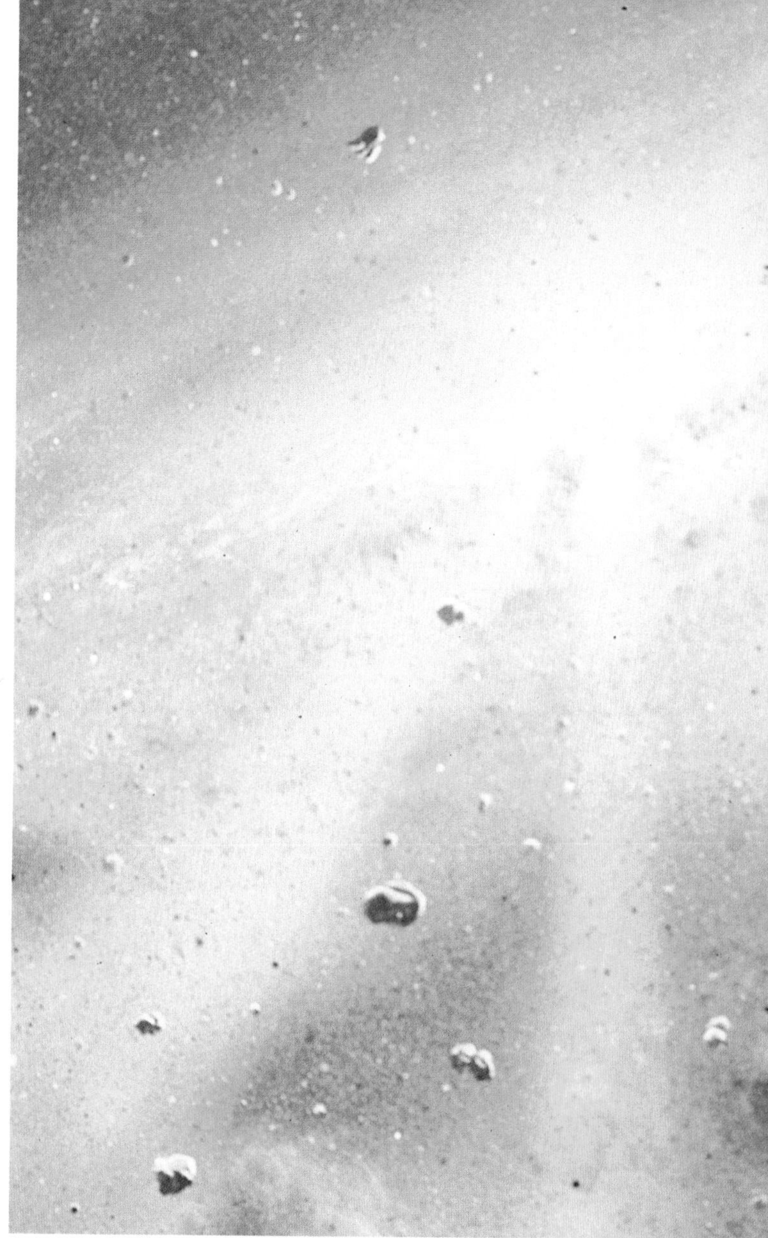

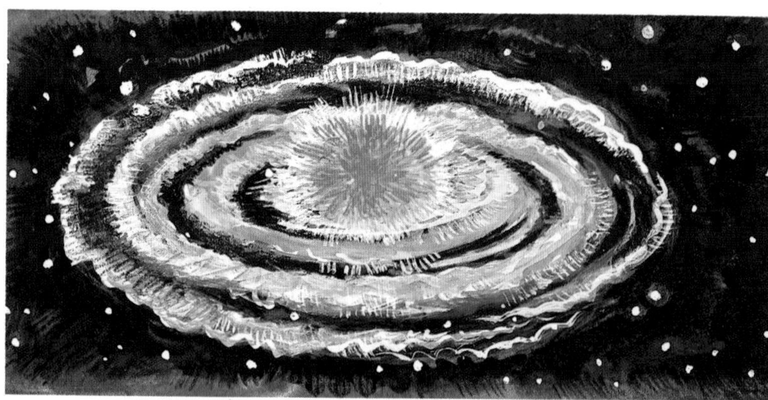

Some 4.6 billion years ago, a small pocket of gas and dust began contracting. Spinning ever faster as it collapsed, the cloud flattened into a disk. For the next ten million years, a contracting ball of gas in the center of the cloud grew smaller, denser, and hotter.

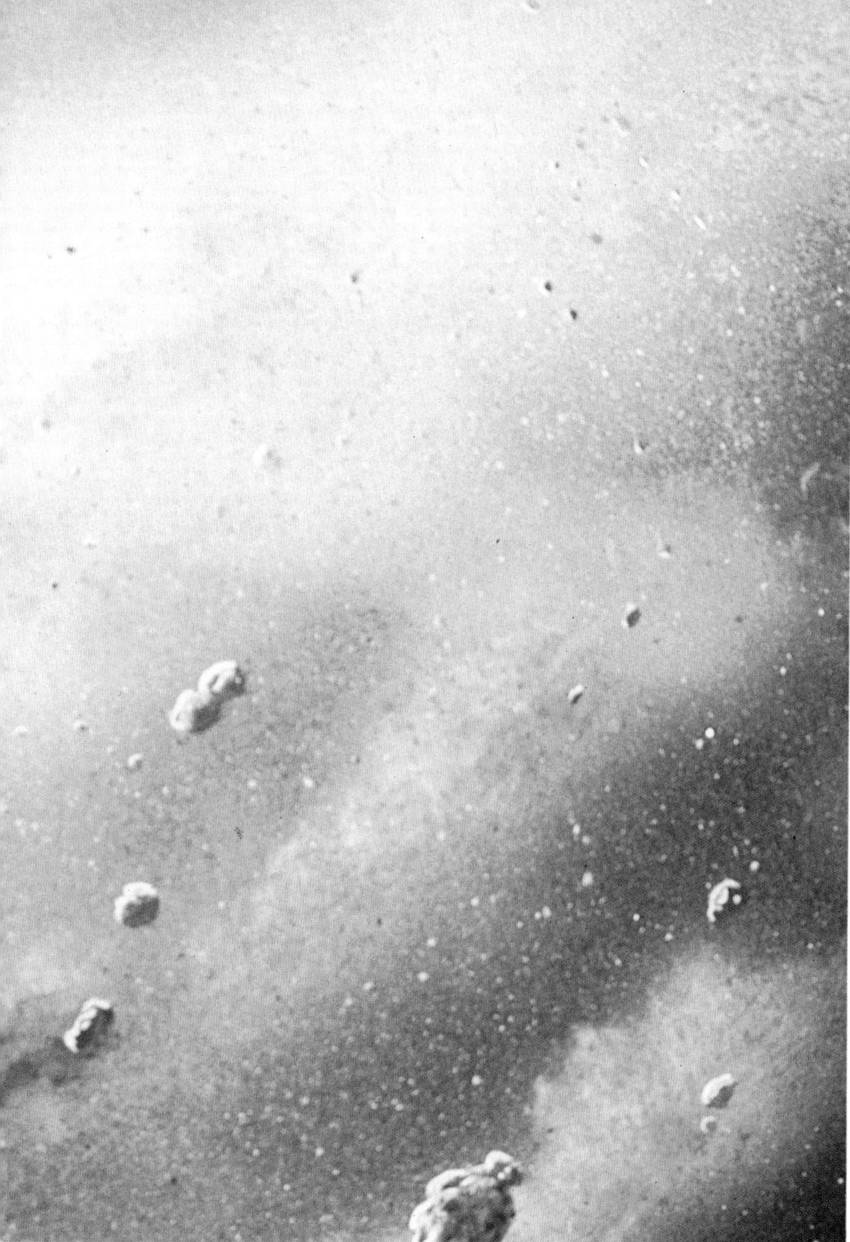

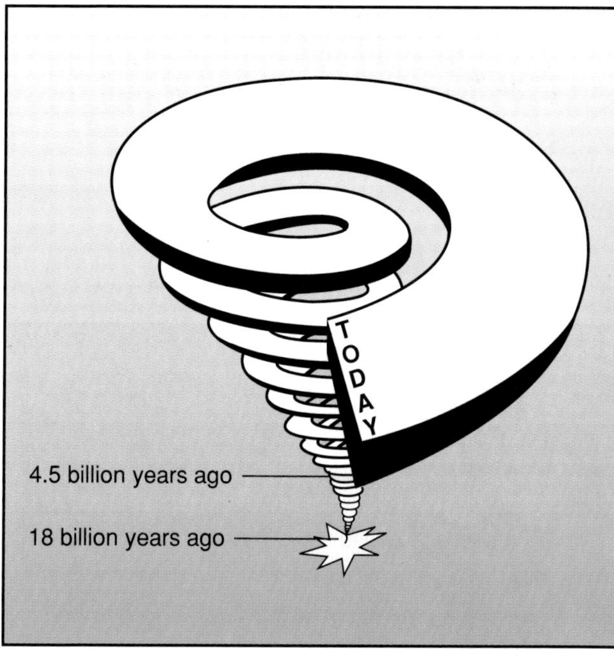

The solar system formed about 4.5 billion years ago.

The young solar system was filled with gas, dust, and small rocky bodies. By colliding and combining, these objects built the planets of the solar system.

The ball then grew hot enough to create helium and energy from hydrogen—the Sun was born. Matter in the disk slowly clumped together, forming the cores of the planets.

Over the next 100 million years, the planets swept up much of the solar system's rocky debris.

Hostile World

The young Earth grew more massive as its gravity drew large chunks of rocky debris into it. These collisions, along with a supply of radioactive elements, generated enough heat to turn the early Earth into a soupy, glowing ball of molten rock and metal. The Earth simmered at a temperature near 2,500° F (1,370° C).

Sometime early in its history the Earth was joined by its partner in space, the Moon. Just how this occurred no one knows, but many scientists believe that a tremendous collision was responsible. The young Earth may have nearly shattered when an object about the size of the planet Mars slammed into it. Some of the material blasted from the Earth remained in orbit and slowly collected into the Moon.

Within 100 million years after the Earth condensed out of a gas cloud, it underwent a

process that forever changed its interior. Molten drops of iron and other heavy elements slowly sank toward the Earth's center. The ball of liquid iron they formed became the Earth's *core*. The core is still mostly liquid today, and its heat drives volcanoes and other geologic activity.

Just as the heavy materials sank into the center of the Earth, lighter elements such as aluminum and silicon floated toward the surface. They collected into large solid masses to form the Earth's outermost layer, called its *crust*.

This early crust could not last long. Heavy bombardment from debris in the young solar system must have smashed it many times. Gradually, strong, stable rocks, such as granite, formed the foundations of the present-day continents.

Now a great glowing ball of molten rock and metal, the young Earth continued its growth by attracting and absorbing smaller bodies. Heat from the impacts helped keep the Earth molten.

Many scientists believe the Moon was born in a cosmic collision. The young Earth may have nearly shattered when an object the size of Mars smashed into it. Debris from the collision was thrown into orbit around the Earth and later collected to form the Moon.

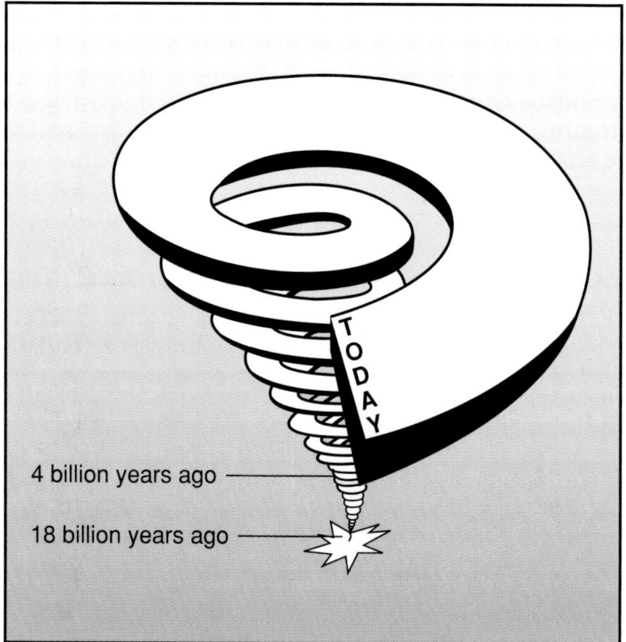

By about 4.5 billion years ago, the Earth's core and crust had formed. The oldest rocks ever discovered are 3.96 billion years old, and the earliest evidence of life appears in 3.5-billion-year-old rock.

The overall heating of Earth's interior marked the beginning of volcanic activity and the building of mountains. Huge outpourings of lava thickened the planet's crust. This in turn helped create Earth's atmosphere. Gases locked in the material that formed the Earth began to bubble up to the planet's surface. Carbon dioxide, methane, and water vapor streamed out of erupting volcanoes.

Water vapor climbed high in the early atmosphere, condensed into water droplets, formed thick clouds, and fell as heavy rains. When the rains hit hot spots on the surface, the water evaporated, condensed, then fell again. The Earth's surface cooled. Its deepest basins filled with water, forming the first oceans.

In these early seas on the young Earth, lightning and strong ultraviolet light from the Sun helped forge complex chemical substances. Some of these chemicals, those known as *amino acids,* are part of the language of life on Earth. Over eons of time, the molecules built from these chemicals became increasingly complex. One day, perhaps

A break in sulfurous clouds reveals the Moon looming over lava pools on the fiery young Earth. The last rain of colliding meteoroids has not yet given the Moon its familiar face. Lava and gases bubble to the Earth's surface, thickening its crust and creating an atmosphere.

within some quiet tidal pool, chance combinations created a molecule with a curious spiral shape and a unique feature: it could make copies of itself. Less than a billion years after Earth's formation, a substance called *DNA* had formed. It is nothing less than the chemical blueprint for life on this planet.

Even as this was happening, the Earth received its last great bombardment, one that would leave the Moon and planets with most of the scars seen today. Perhaps the fragile beginnings of life were blasted away several times, only to form again and again.

THE LIVING PLANET

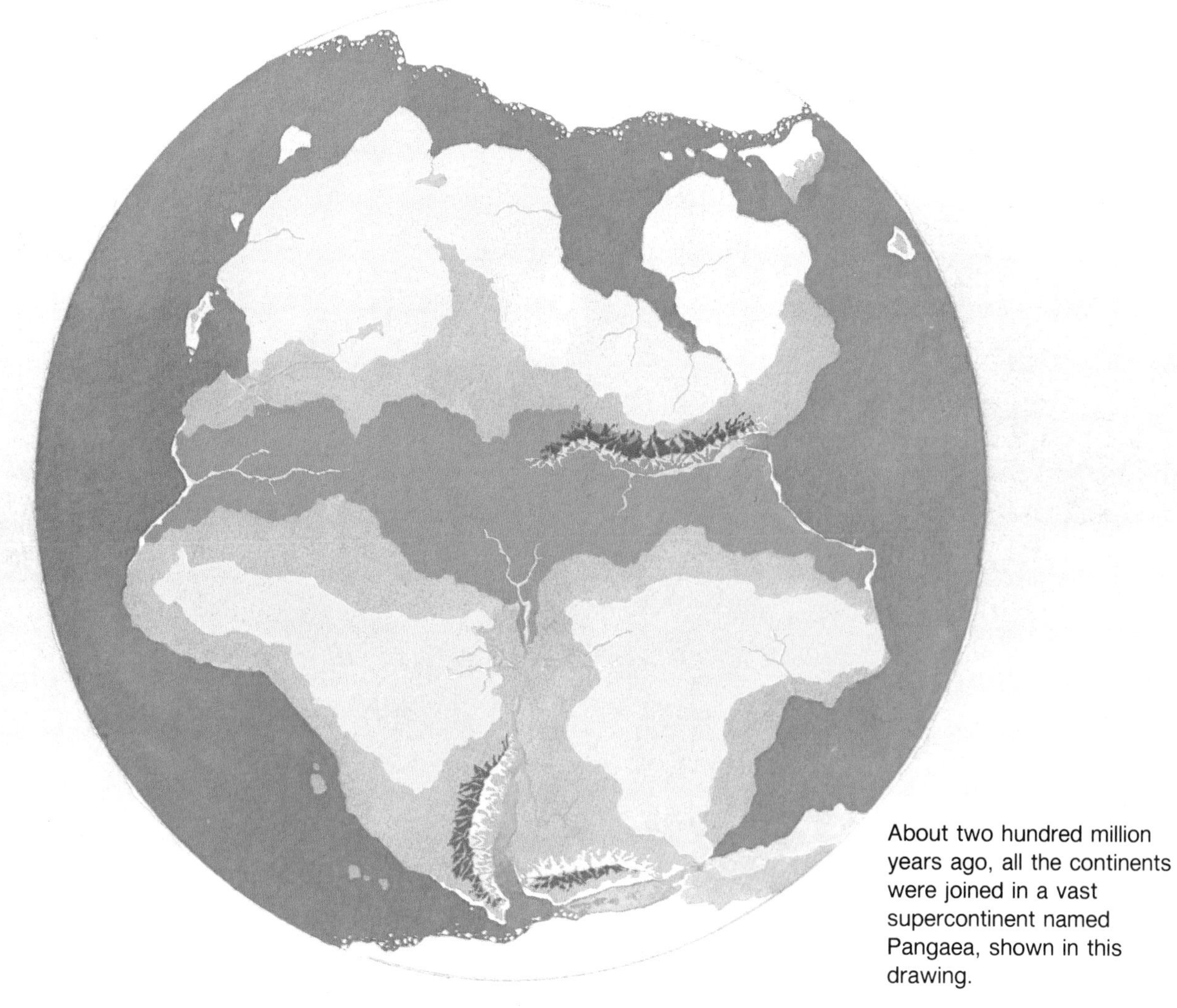

About two hundred million years ago, all the continents were joined in a vast supercontinent named Pangaea, shown in this drawing.

The Faces of Earth

Even today, some 4.5 billion years after the Earth formed, its surface has still not settled down. In fact, the changing nature of Earth's surface is a feature that makes it unique among all the planets in the solar system.

The crust, Earth's outermost shell of rock, is not a continuous layer. It is broken into a dozen or so large, rigid slabs geologists call *tectonic plates.* These plates slide against one another at speeds between about 0.4 and 4 inches (1 and 10 centimeters) per year. Plates are thicker under the continents than under the ocean, but they average about fifty miles (eighty kilometers) thick. They are formed out of the Earth's crust and the topmost portion of the Earth's interior. This upper layer is called the *mantle.*

The plates slide atop a layer of the deeper mantle. Here the rock is hot enough and

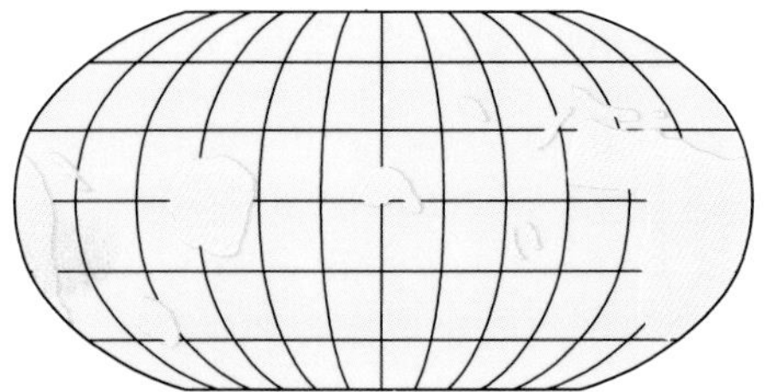

The Earth's surface as it appeared about 510 million years ago...

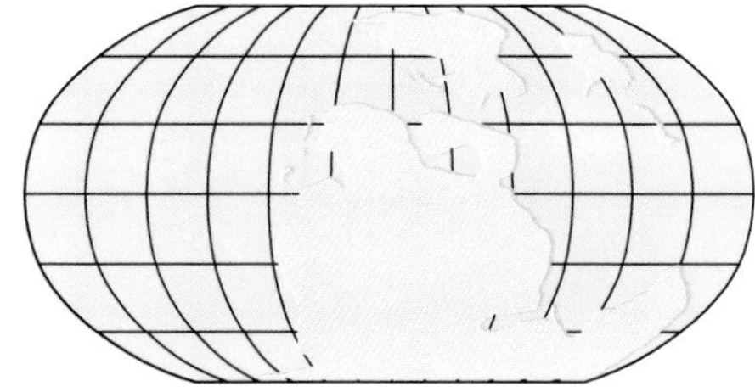

...about 240 million years ago...

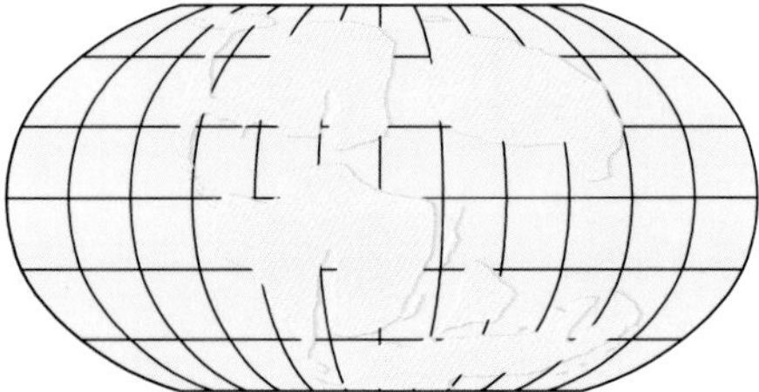

...about 135 million years ago...

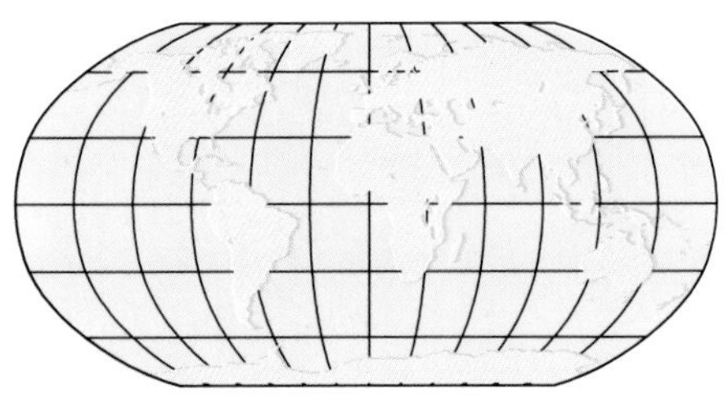

...and as it appears today.

The movement of tectonic plates accounts for all of the Earth's geologic activity: volcanoes erupt above hot spots where one plate rides over another (below left); mountains build when plates crash together; earthquakes release the tension when plates grind past each other (below right). The movement of plates also changes the arrangement of Earth's land masses over time.

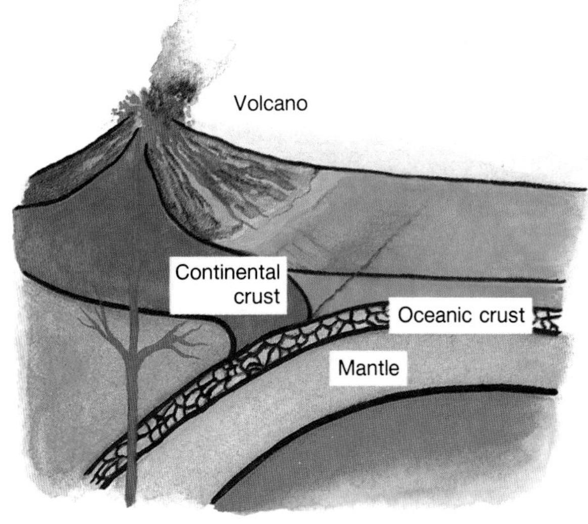

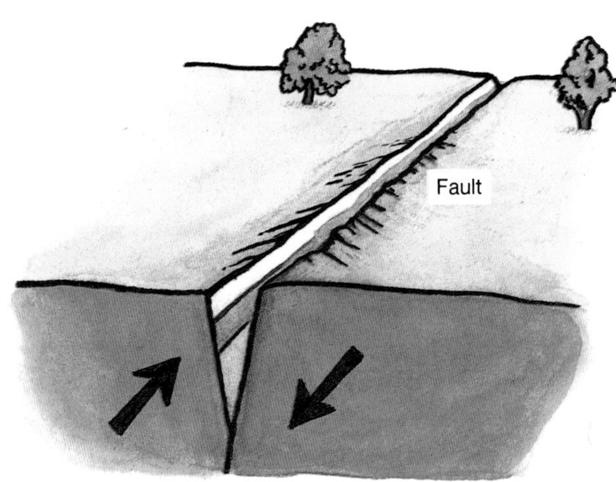

weak enough to swirl as a result of heat rising from still deeper parts of the interior. These swirling currents nudge the plates. Stress builds up where plates grind against each other, relieved only when rock shatters and creates earthquakes. Near a plate boundary, molten rock rises to the surface and erupts along cracks to form volcanoes.

The Earth's moving tectonic plates also change the size and arrangement of land masses. Hot rock wells up at undersea ridges along the boundaries of plates, adding material to the sea floor and widening the oceans. In other areas, a plate may be destroyed as it slides under another. The face of Earth changes over time, and much of the evidence of its distant past has been destroyed by this activity.

The Story of Rocks

The task of charting Earth's distant past seems difficult, but it is one of the most exciting in all of science. The record of Earth's past is held within its rocks. Over the past four hundred years, scientists have struggled to learn to read that record.

People have long collected strange or interesting pieces of rock. Sometimes rocks far from the sea would take on shapes that looked much like shells or underwater plants. Today, such rocks are known to be the petrified remains of plants or animals and are called *fossils*. Even as early as 1500, many argued that fossils were exactly what they appeared to be. Leonardo da Vinci, the famous sixteenth-century Italian artist, wrote as much in his notebooks.

For a hundred years, scientists engaged in a lively debate over the origin and meaning of fossils. The English scientist Robert Hooke

Horizontal stripes running along the walls of Arizona's Grand Canyon represent layers of rock that formed at different times. Long ago, when the area was submerged beneath a vast sea, sediments sank to the seafloor and turned into rock. The Colorado River later carved a path through the rock, creating the canyon and revealing its layered walls.

Scientists at Dinosaur National Monument in Utah carefully extract the jumbled remains of ancient animals from their resting place in sandstone. The wall contains over two thousand fossil bones.

believed that fossils were of animal origin. So did the Danish physician Nicolaus Steno.

In 1666, Steno was living in Florence, Italy. He became interested in fossils after local fishermen brought him a large white shark they had caught. Steno noticed a similarity between the triangular teeth of the shark and a type of triangular rock then known as "tonguestones."

Steno suggested that the tonguestones really *were* the teeth of ancient sharks. How could shark's teeth and other sea creatures turn into solid rock? Steno suggested that one type of rock formed over a long period of time at the bottom of a river or ocean. As the rock formed, he thought, animals or parts of them were trapped within it.

Buried for 145 million years, the massive shoulder blade of an *Apatosaurus* and other fossils are at last unearthed.

The type of rock Steno considered is called *sedimentary* rock. In 1669, he suggested that such rock formed under lakes, rivers, or oceans as silt and sand fell to the bottom. It collected in layers, with the youngest layers on top and older layers on the bottom. This discovery enabled scientists to learn the order in which geologic events occurred.

The best examples of sedimentary rock are the colorful, banded walls of the Grand Canyon in Arizona. There the flow of the Colorado River has cut through and exposed ever-deeper layers of rock. Rock layers at the bottom of the canyon formed first, and higher layers formed later.

Such orderly rock layers, or *strata,* are an exception. The slow but ceaseless changes of the Earth's surface can turn well-organized layers of rock into a complex jumble. In some places, wind and rain have worn away the uppermost rock layers. Nowhere on Earth are there intact rock layers that reflect a major portion of Earth's history. The confusing jumble of layers from different periods found all over the world make it difficult to piece together an overall picture of Earth's past.

To early theorists, fossils provided a key to unlocking the mystery of the Earth's past. In the late 1700s, an English civil engineer named William Smith found that particular kinds of fossils occurred only in certain types of rock. Finding the same kinds of fossils in

Preserved by the ash of an erupting volcano, this fish helps tell the story of Earth's past.

This robber fly buzzed around Florrisant, Colorado, some 35 million years ago.

The fossil at upper left of an ancient shark's tooth looks very much like the teeth of living sharks. The series above shows how fossils form. A dinosaur dies in a river or a lake and sinks to the muddy bottom (figure 1). Layers of sediment bury the dinosaur. Its flesh decays, but the sediment layers help preserve its bones (figure 2). The lake slowly evaporates over millions of years. The muddy lake bed dries out and turns to rock (figure 3). Eventually, wind and rain wear away parts of this sedimentary rock, revealing the fossilized bones of the dinosaur (figure 4).

layers of rock from widely different locations meant that the rock at those places probably formed at the same time. Scientists also noticed that fossils found in older, lower rock layers looked very different from living things. This suggested that whatever creatures the fossils represented had lived a very long time ago. Fossils in younger rock closely resembled plants or animals still living, which meant that the remains were relatively recent. So fossils provided scientists with a way to identify the relative ages of rock layers around the world.

By comparing fossil information in rock layers throughout the world, geologists assembled an overall picture of the sequence of rock layers, from the youngest to the oldest. This general picture is called the *geologic column.* Although geologists could determine which of two rock layers formed first, they still did not know how long the layer took to form. They had no idea of how much time the geologic column represented. Imagine how a historian might feel knowing that the American Revolution had occurred before World War II, but not knowing the years in which the wars took place. Throughout the 1800s, scientists argued over how fast Earth's changes occur.

In the 1890s, scientists discovered that the atoms of certain elements were unstable. They spontaneously change, or decay, into lighter elements, sending out streams of subatomic particles and energy in the process. Materials that behave this way are called *radioactive.* Radioactive elements include polonium, radium, and uranium.

Furthermore, scientists learned that half of the atoms in a rock containing the most common form of uranium will decay into a form of lead over a period of about 4.5 billion years. This period is known as the *half-life* of uranium.

Not long after the discovery of radioactivity, a few scientists realized that such materials might serve as a kind of "atomic clock" for finding the ages of rocks. By comparing the amount of uranium in a rock sample to the amount of decay product (lead), scientists could calculate how much time had passed since the rock formed.

Geologists had divided the Earth's past into four eras based on the fossils found within the different rock layers. These were called the Cenozoic, Mesozoic, Paleozoic, and the Precambrian. Each era (except the Precambrian) was further divided into periods, again based on the fossil record. Geologists knew that rocks from the Cambrian Period of the Paleozoic Era held the first abundant fossils. But they still did not know how long ago the creatures had lived.

Dating techniques using radioactive materials provided the answer. Today scientists use several dating methods, which employ different radioactive materials. The oldest rocks ever found on Earth, discovered in northern Canada in 1989, have been dated as 3.96 billion years old. Rocks collected from the Moon in the early 1970s solidified between 3.7 billion and 4.5 billion years ago. And the oldest signs of life on Earth were molded into Australian rocks some 3.5 billion years ago.

Based on the radioactive decay of elements, "atomic clocks" enable scientists to determine the actual age of rocks and the fossils they contain. Over 4.5 billion years, half of the uranium in a rock sample turns into one form of lead. By comparing the amount of uranium and lead in the rock, scientists can find its age. Other radioactive elements useful in dating materials include forms of carbon, thorium, and potassium.

◆ Lead atoms

● Uranium atoms

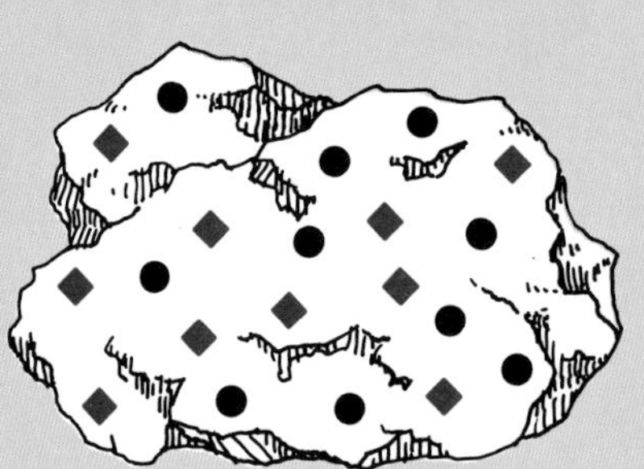

This rock is 4.5 billion years old. The diamonds and circles show relative number of uranium and lead atoms it contains.

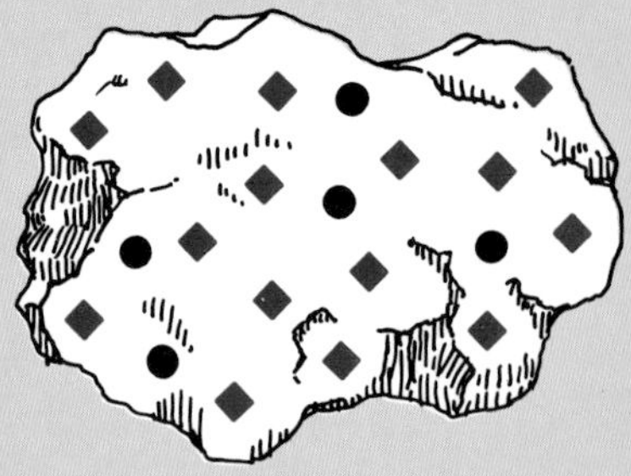

After another 4.5 billion years has passed, half of the rock's uranium atoms have decayed into lead atoms.

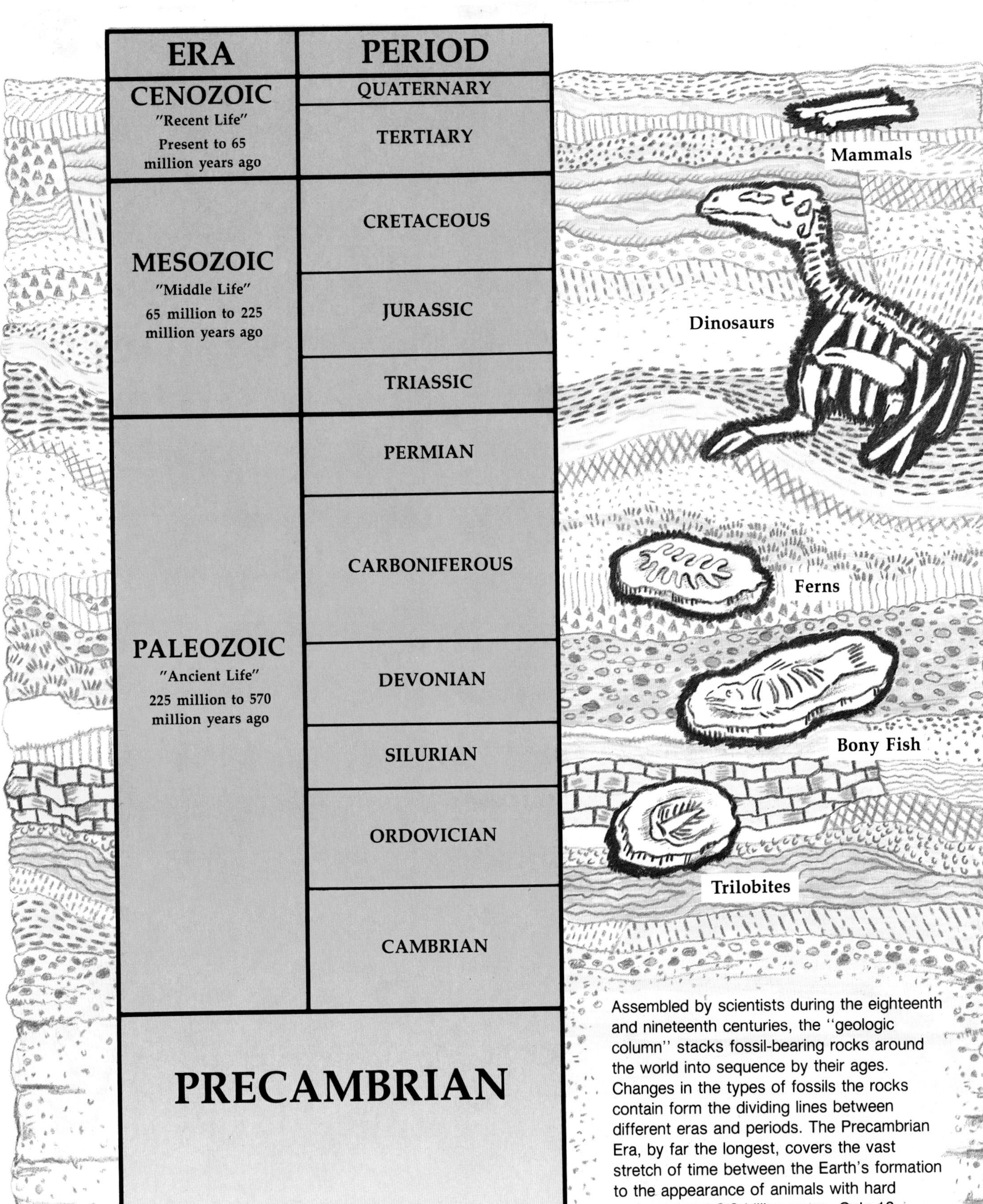

ERA
PERIOD
CENOZOIC
"Recent Life"
Present to 65 million years ago
QUATERNARY
TERTIARY
MESOZOIC
"Middle Life"
65 million to 225 million years ago
CRETACEOUS
JURASSIC
TRIASSIC
PALEOZOIC
"Ancient Life"
225 million to 570 million years ago
PERMIAN
CARBONIFEROUS
DEVONIAN
SILURIAN
ORDOVICIAN
CAMBRIAN
PRECAMBRIAN
Mammals
Dinosaurs
Ferns
Bony Fish
Trilobites

Assembled by scientists during the eighteenth and nineteenth centuries, the "geologic column" stacks fossil-bearing rocks around the world into sequence by their ages. Changes in the types of fossils the rocks contain form the dividing lines between different eras and periods. The Precambrian Era, by far the longest, covers the vast stretch of time between the Earth's formation to the appearance of animals with hard parts—about 3.9 billion years. Only 13 percent of Earth's history is revealed in the fossil record.

Precambrian: The Earliest Life

Within Earth's first billion years, its crust cooled and solidified. Vast oceans filled the largest basins, and a poisonous atmosphere enveloped the planet. The rain of giant meteorites, whose devastating impacts put the finishing touches on the faces of the planets, began a gradual decline. Intense ultraviolet sunlight sterilized the young Earth's barren, rocky surface.

Virtually no life today could exist under such conditions, yet this is where life began. By about 3.4 billion years ago, simple single-cell microscopic plants such as blue-green algae probably filled the oceans. Instead of absorbing nutrients from the sea around them, these plants made their own food by using the energy in sunlight. The process, called *photosynthesis,* fuels virtually all plant life today.

Ancient rock formations called *stromatolites* reveal the existence of blue-green algae communities, whose sticky mats create the layered rocks by trapping sand and mud. Stromatolites dominate the fossil record for the next 2.7 billion years, and still exist today. Sponges, worms, jellyfish-like creatures, and other simple animals did not appear until about 700 million years ago. The miraculous explosion of life on Earth was underway.

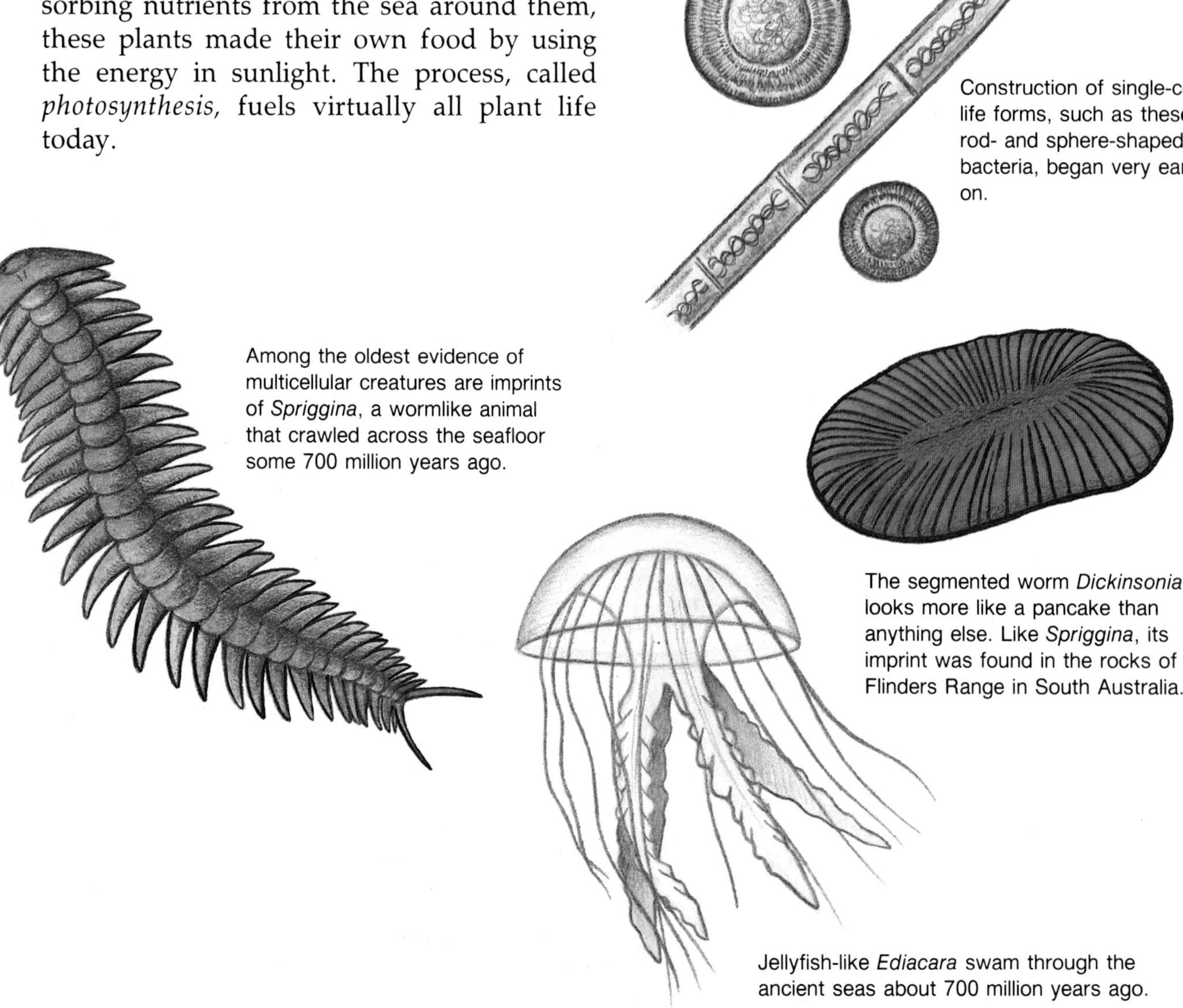

Construction of single-celled life forms, such as these rod- and sphere-shaped bacteria, began very early on.

Among the oldest evidence of multicellular creatures are imprints of *Spriggina*, a wormlike animal that crawled across the seafloor some 700 million years ago.

The segmented worm *Dickinsonia* looks more like a pancake than anything else. Like *Spriggina*, its imprint was found in the rocks of Flinders Range in South Australia.

Jellyfish-like *Ediacara* swam through the ancient seas about 700 million years ago.

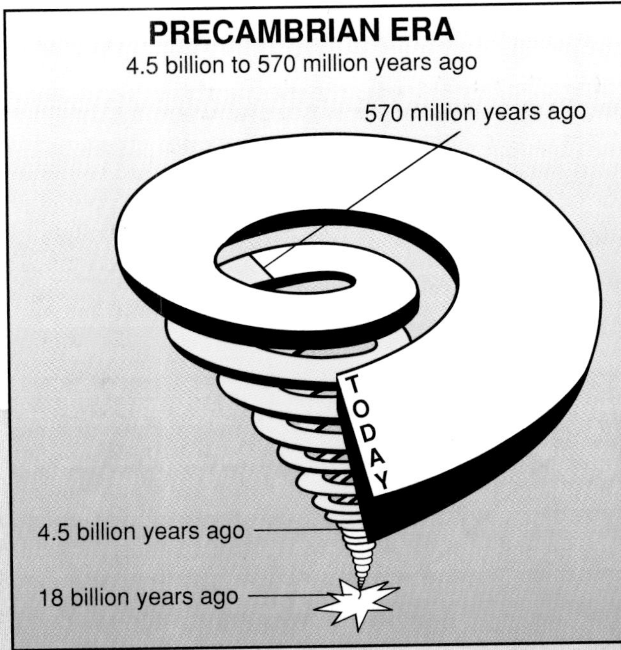

The Precambrian Era spans the four billion years between Earth's formation and the appearance of marine animals with hard body parts.

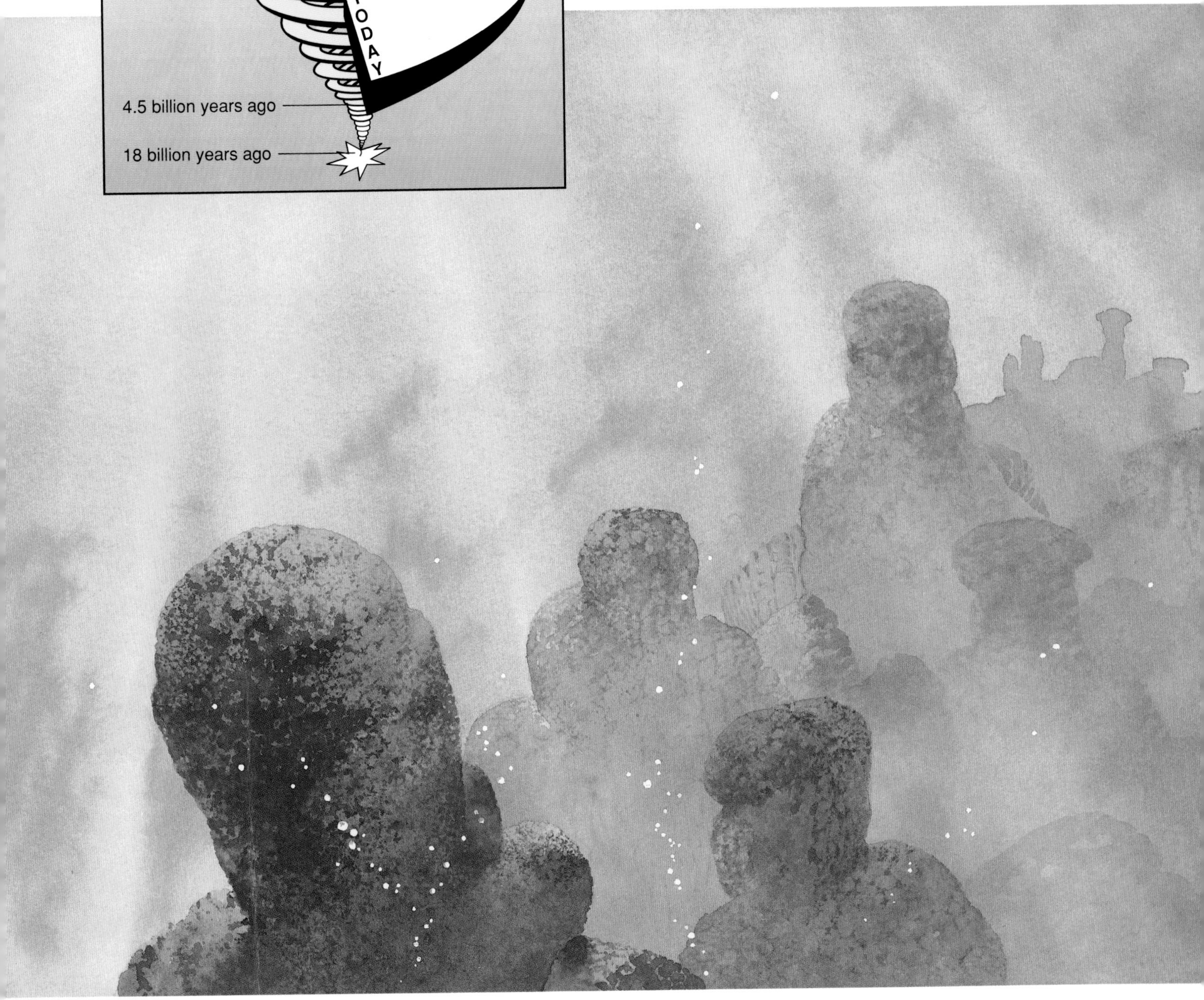

Sticky mats of blue-green algae create large dome-shaped structures called stromatolites. Filaments on the mat's upper surface trap mud particles, which become solidified into layered domes. A few stromatolites exist today, but they dominate the fossil record between three billion and 700 million years ago.

THE PALEOZOIC ERA

The Age of Undersea Invertebrates

Rocks from the Cambrian Period, some 570 million years old, reveal an explosion of diversity of life. Earlier soft-bodied, or *invertebrate,* creatures—such as worms or jellyfish—make only rare appearances as fossils because only very special conditions can preserve their remains. But at the close of the Precambrian Era, animals with hard external skeletons began to appear. Since the hard skeleton was easier to preserve, the life forms of the Cambrian Period provide scientists with abundant specimens to study.

One of the most common creatures found in Cambrian rock are the *trilobites.* These oval-shaped animals usually lived on the seafloor, scurrying through the mud to find food. They ranged in size from smaller than an inch (2.5 centimeters) to well over a foot (31 centimeters). If threatened, they protected themselves by rolling into a tight ball.

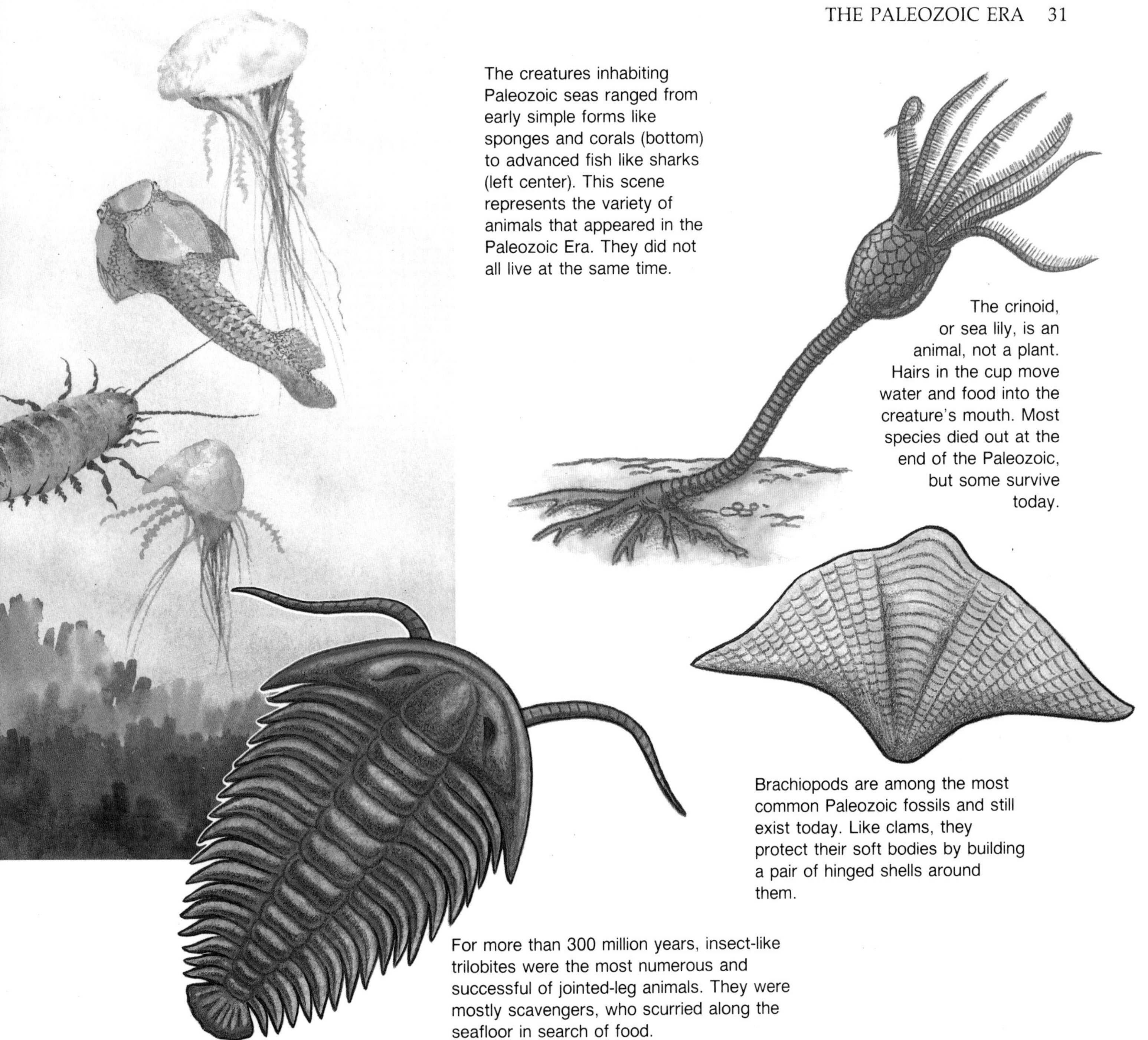

The creatures inhabiting Paleozoic seas ranged from early simple forms like sponges and corals (bottom) to advanced fish like sharks (left center). This scene represents the variety of animals that appeared in the Paleozoic Era. They did not all live at the same time.

The crinoid, or sea lily, is an animal, not a plant. Hairs in the cup move water and food into the creature's mouth. Most species died out at the end of the Paleozoic, but some survive today.

Brachiopods are among the most common Paleozoic fossils and still exist today. Like clams, they protect their soft bodies by building a pair of hinged shells around them.

For more than 300 million years, insect-like trilobites were the most numerous and successful of jointed-leg animals. They were mostly scavengers, who scurried along the seafloor in search of food.

Other animals, called *crinoids,* sat rooted to the sea floor by long stems. A crinoid's mouth, surrounded by five or more arms, sat within a cup at the stem's top. The arms circulated water, bringing food to the animal's mouth. *Brachiopods,* marine mollusks contained within clam-like shells, also fed with the help of small, fine tentacles. Crinoids and brachiopods can still be found today.

Alongside these familiar forms in Cambrian fossils are some of nature's more bizarre experiments. One creature, called *Opabinia,* had five eyes fixed on short stalks and a long spiked "nozzle" for snatching prey. Another, known as *Hallucigenia,* strutted the seafloor on seven pairs of rigid legs with seven tentacles waving from its back. *Anomalocaris,* a large predator with a circular mouth, died out by the end of the Cambrian—long before its trilobite prey became extinct.

The Ordovician Period began 510 million years ago and lasted about eighty million years. During this time marine invertebrates dramatically increased their numbers and expanded into new environments. Life flourished in the warm tropical seas that covered northern Europe and the eastern United States.

Flower-like crinoids writhed on their stalks, secured firmly to rocks on the muddy sea bottom. Trilobites of all sizes appeared in most marine environments. A few corals appeared. *Cephalopods,* the ancestors of the modern squid and octopus, were represented. Their shells were sometimes straight cones from which the creature's soft parts—eyes and arms—extended. Other types had curved shells, similar to the chambered nautilus that exists today.

An altogether new creature appeared in the Ordovician Period: a primitive fish. These were the first true *vertebrates,* or animals with backbones. Their large armored heads earned

Sponges date from the last part of the Precambrian Era, some 700 million years ago. They represent one of the oldest and simplest examples of animal life.

The cephalopods called *nautiloids* introduced a new life-style in Ordovician seas. They became active hunters, able to speed through the seas with a special water jet. One straight-shelled nautiloid, *Endoceras,* could grow twelve feet (3.6 meters) in length. Other types had curved and even coiled shells.

Life in the Ordovician seas included some forms familiar in today's seas, such as snails and corals. Multi-armed cephalopods (right), trilobites (upper left), brachiopods (middle right), and the spindly sea scorpion (middle left) ruled the seafloor.

them the name *ostracoderms,* which means "bony shield." These early fish had powerful tails but lacked fins that could take them high above the seafloor. They must have fed by plowing along the sea bottom, sifting through the mud with their circular, jawless mouths. The stage was set for the Age of Fishes.

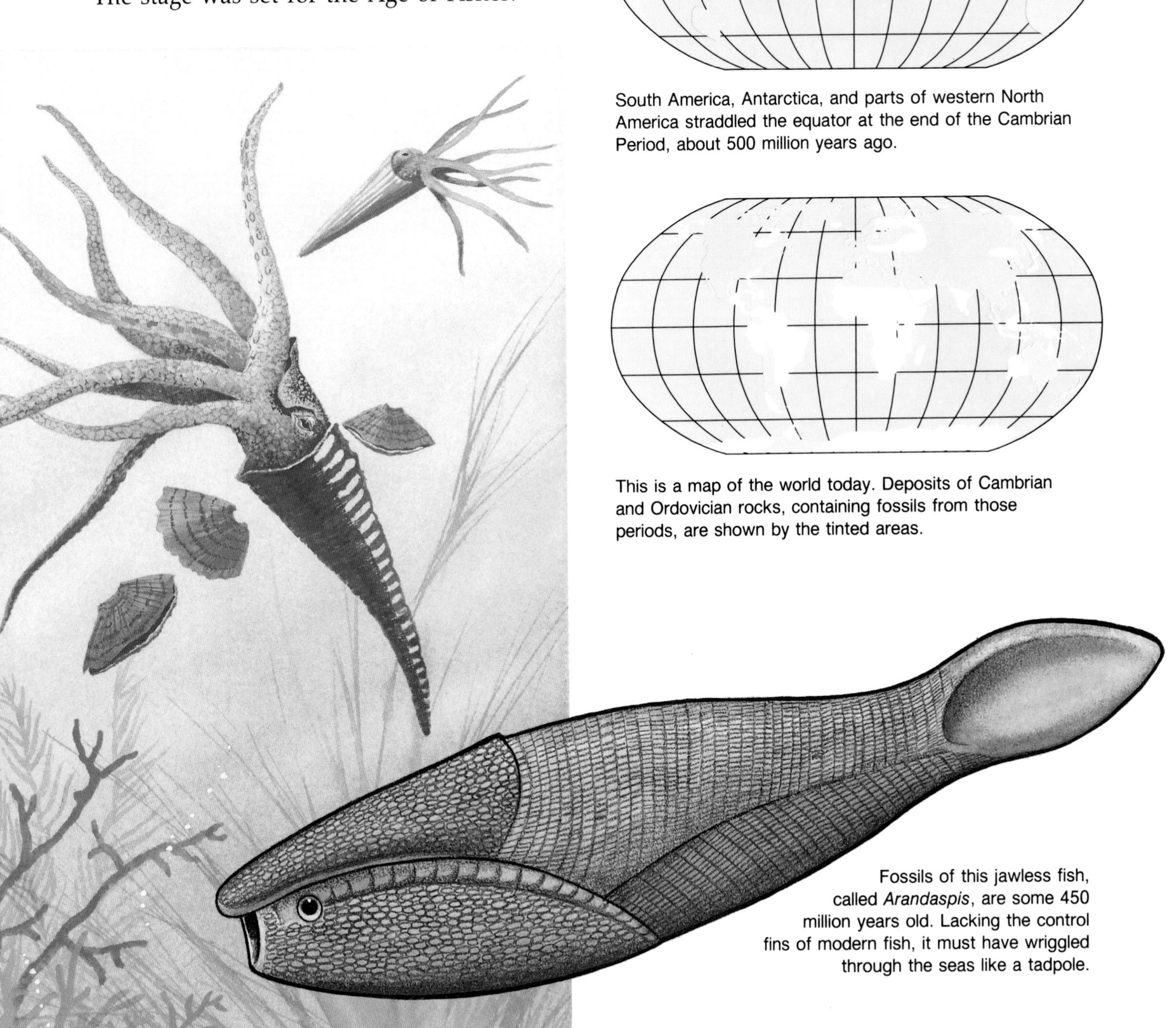

South America, Antarctica, and parts of western North America straddled the equator at the end of the Cambrian Period, about 500 million years ago.

This is a map of the world today. Deposits of Cambrian and Ordovician rocks, containing fossils from those periods, are shown by the tinted areas.

Fossils of this jawless fish, called *Arandaspis*, are some 450 million years old. Lacking the control fins of modern fish, it must have wriggled through the seas like a tadpole.

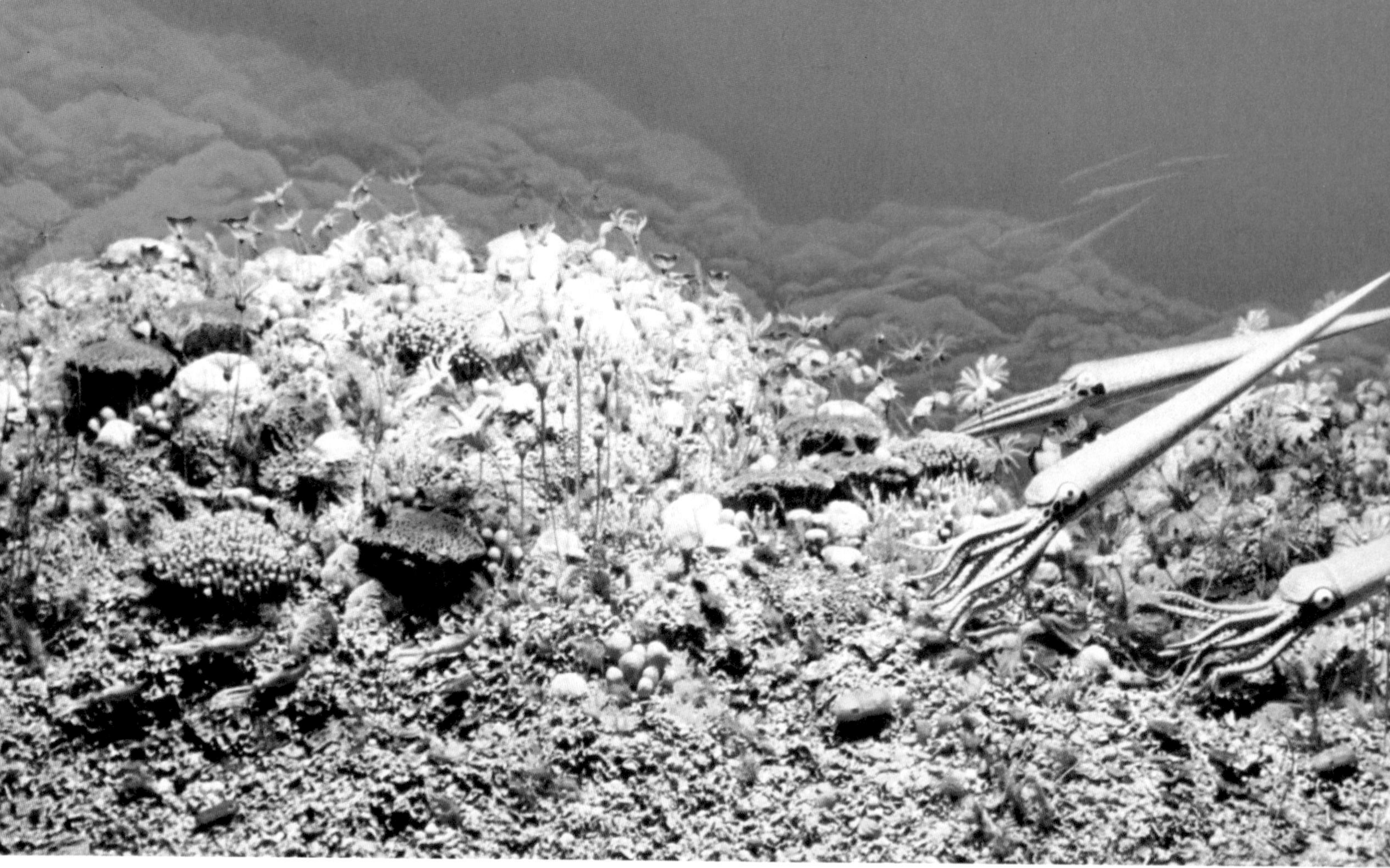

In the warm, shallow seas of the Silurian Period, coral reefs attracted all kinds of animals. Hungry cephalopods search for a meal along a reef that will become part of Wisconsin some 400 million years later.

The Age of Fishes

During the Silurian Period, between 430 and 395 million years ago, Africa and South America capped the Earth's south pole while North America and parts of Europe sat on the equator. Life flourished in the warm, shallow seas. Full-fledged coral reefs and the complex communities they support appeared.

Oddly, the primitive fish ostracoderm vanished from the fossil record after 60 million years of success. This coincided with the appearance of the *placoderms* ("plate-skinned"), the world's oldest true fish. With them came a weapon no ostracoderm could battle: the jaw. For the remaining years of the Silurian Period, placoderms hunted down and wiped out their own ancestors. The jawed killers ruled the sea.

For the more than three billion years in which life had existed on Earth, it remained locked in the world's oceans. In the warm, humid climate of the Silurian, however, life finally took to the land. Plants led the way.

When plants make their food by photosynthesis, they release oxygen gas. Over the eons, as plants released oxygen into the oceans, the gas also built up in the atmosphere. High above the oceans, some of the oxygen formed a layer of ozone gas. Ozone

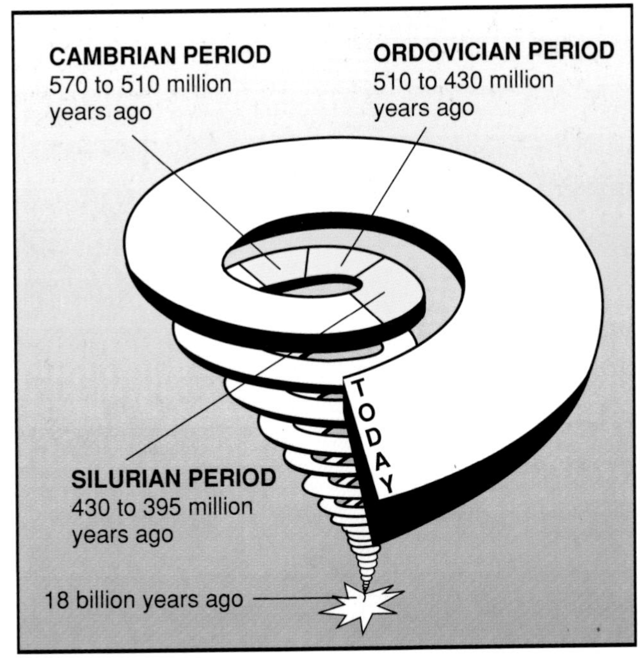

Over the millions of years of the Cambrian, Ordovician, and Silurian periods, nature's experiments produced the backbone and jaw. The next step: the move onto land.

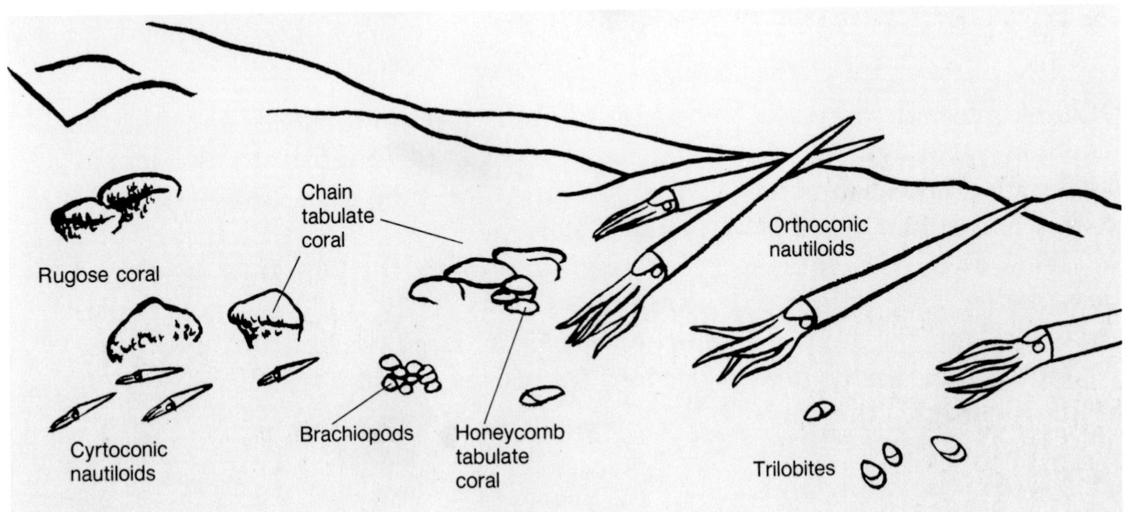

This is a key to the Silurian reef illustration (above left). Typical life forms from the Silurian Period are labeled.

screens out the Sun's harmful rays, and the creation of an ozone layer meant that life could now exist on land.

Perhaps it began with small patches of algae on shoreline rocks, repeatedly exposed to the air as tides rose and fell. Regardless of how it happened, though, the earliest known land plants had appeared by 410 million years ago. At first they clustered around the water's edge, but gradually they spread throughout the interiors of the continents.

Lobe-finned fish like this coelacanth were the first vertebrates to tackle the land, breathing air and waddling to new ponds on strong, muscular fins some 350 million years ago. They were considered extinct until 1938, when one was caught off the coast of South Africa.

During the Devonian Period, between 395 and 345 million years ago, plants spread across the landscape. Toward the end of the Devonian, insects make their first appearance in fossils. Living along the shoreline, primitive spiders, mites, and silverfish claimed the landscape for animals. Innovations in the ocean continued as many new fish forms appeared, including the first sharks.

Volcanoes erupted in what is now England, Greenland, western Canada, and the Soviet Union. The world climate, drier than during the Silurian, also grew less predictable. Droughts followed intense rainy periods.

The warmer waters contained less oxygen, and many fish suffocated as water temperatures rose. Some fish, however, could gulp air from the surface and hold it down. Their tiny blood vessels absorbed the oxygen. These fish developed into such creatures as the modern lungfish found in Africa and Australia. Some species of lungfish are so dependent on air that they will drown if held underwater.

One group of fish, the lobe-fins, developed more than lungs. They could lift their bodies up on a pair of large, fleshy fins and, using powerful muscles, waddle from one pond to another.

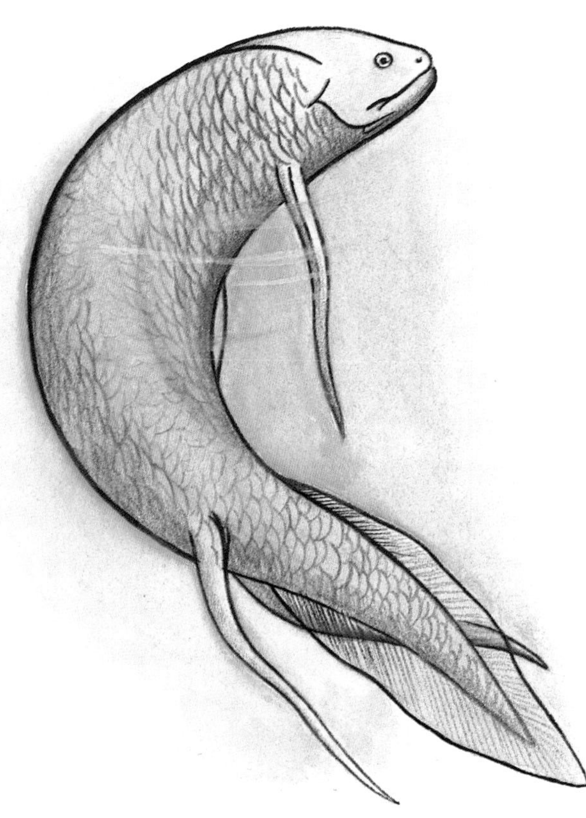

Modern lung-bearing fish, or lungfish, can be found in Australian, African, and South American rivers. Some have both lungs and gills, allowing them to breathe in or out of water, but others will drown if kept from reaching the surface.

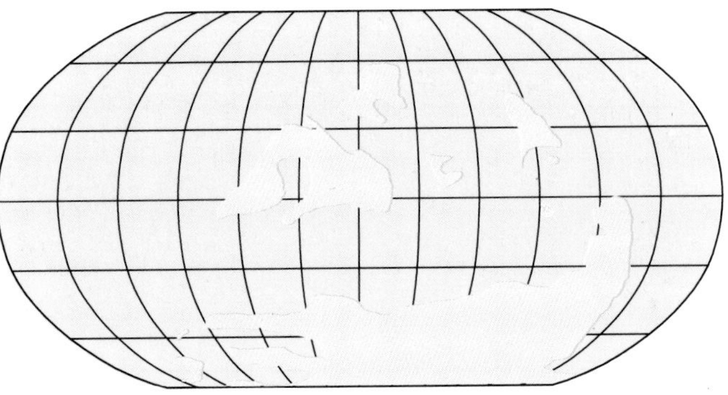

During the Devonian Period, the Earth's south pole lay in central Africa while the equator cut through North America, Greenland, and Europe. This map shows the positions of the continents 390 million years ago.

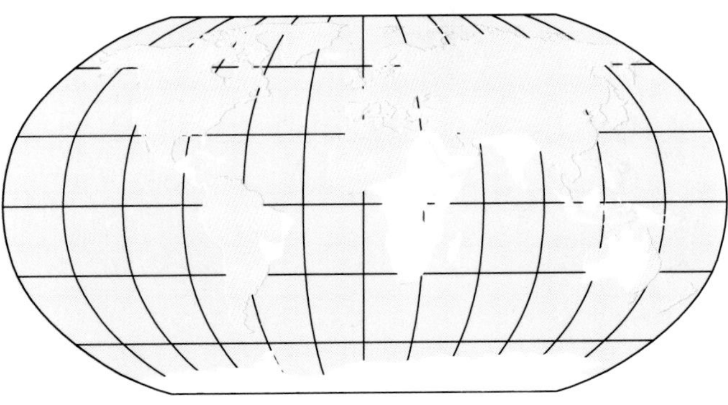

Rocks containing fossils from the mid-Paleozoic are tinted in this map of the world as it is today.

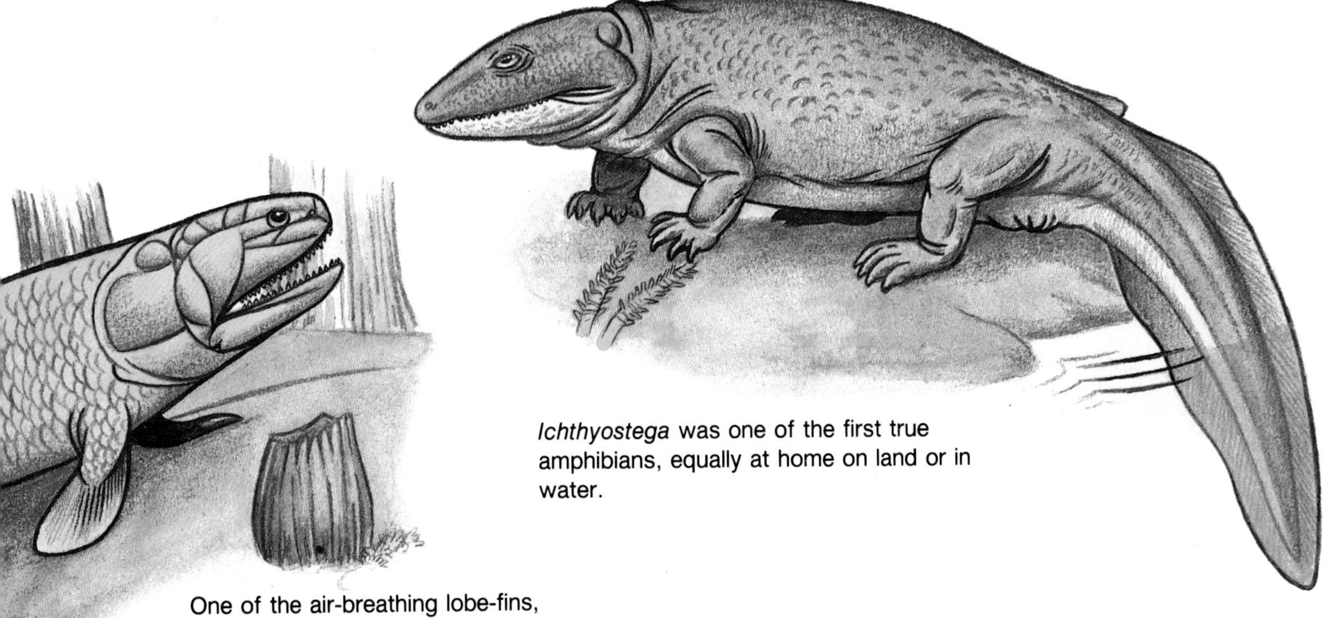

Ichthyostega was one of the first true amphibians, equally at home on land or in water.

One of the air-breathing lobe-fins, *Eusthenopteron* could probably hold its weight on its paired fins and half-drag, half-waddle across the late Devonian landscape.

The Age of Amphibians

The climate turned warm and moist during the Carboniferous Period, 345 million to 270 million years ago. This favorable weather stimulated the conquest of land areas by plants. During the warm, humid Carboniferous, steamy lagoons supported giant club mosses, tree ferns, and calamatids—giant relatives of today's waist-high horsetails. Farther inland, the trees collected into dense forests that covered eastern North America and Europe.

These forests are what give the Carboniferous Period its name. Dense layers of dead vegetation were buried and compressed before they could decay. Over the eons, pressure and heat turned these ancient forest remains into the world's greatest deposits of coal. Quite literally, today's civilization is fueled by the forests of Earth's past.

Insects also flourished during the Carboniferous. The cockroach appeared early on, scurrying along the rotted vegetation it used for food and keeping its distance from *Arthropleura,* a human-sized millipede-like insect. Life took to the air in the Carboniferous as giant dragonflies—often with wingspans

Insects flourish among the enormous tree ferns of a Carboniferous swamp. A giant dragonfly with a wingspan of nearly twenty inches (fifty centimeters) buzzes past a human-sized "millipede." The amphibians crawled out of the water onto shores like this.

Giant ferns and club mosses made up only part of the vast Carboniferous greenery. Shown here is a fossilized portion of a shrub.

greater than one foot (thirty centimeters)—buzzed through the swamps.

One line of amphibians, the *labyrinthodonts,* had teeth similar to those of the lobefins from which they developed. Their diet may have included insects, but they probably relied mostly on fish and other aquatic animals. Despite their success, amphibians were forced to remain near the water's edge, held back both by their food supply and their need to reproduce in water. To expand into the inland world forbidden to amphibians, another type of animal appeared: the reptile.

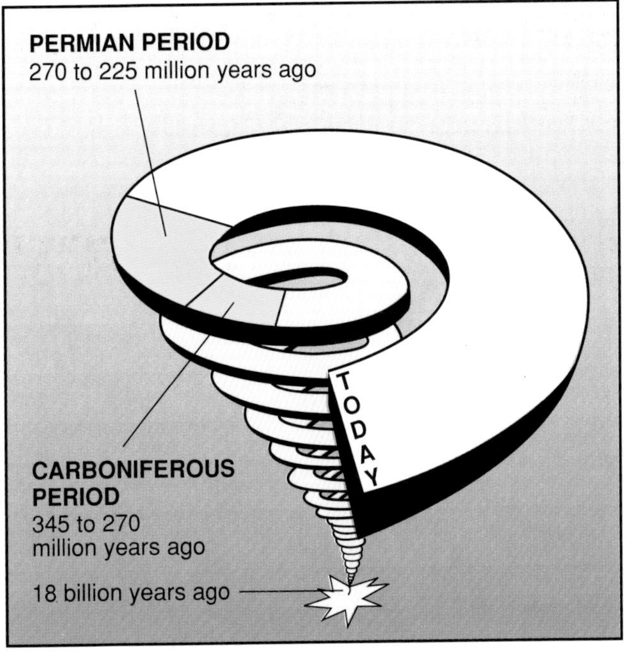

During the Carboniferous and Permian periods, between 345 and 225 million years ago, amphibians and reptiles developed within the vast swamplands and dense forests covering much of North America and Europe.

The gentle folds of the Appalachian Mountains were thrust upward when Africa rammed into North America some 320 million years ago. The collision lasted perhaps fifty million years. The view includes parts of Virginia, West Virginia, and Maryland.

Reptiles were the first creatures to be truly independent from water, the first to live entirely on land. Amphibian eggs, held together by blobs of jelly, dry out unless submerged. Reptile eggs had protective outer coverings that kept them from drying out. As the Carboniferous ended and the Permian Period opened, the climate turned drier. Many land masses were also rising, draining the lagoons and swamps that served amphibians so well. As forests turned to deserts, many amphibian forms disappeared.

Reptiles, on the other hand, underwent an explosion of diversity. Meat-eaters, plant-eaters, and whole new families of animals appeared as life took advantage of new opportunities. Some of these odder varieties are referred to as "mammal-like" reptiles, or *therapsids. Dimetrodon,* a four-legged carnivore found in Texas, is an example. Unlike

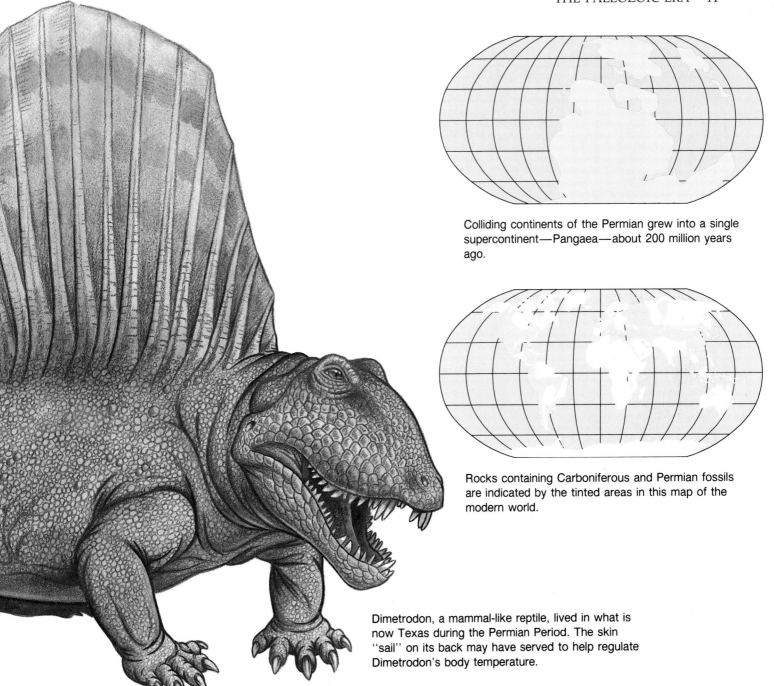

Colliding continents of the Permian grew into a single supercontinent—Pangaea—about 200 million years ago.

Rocks containing Carboniferous and Permian fossils are indicated by the tinted areas in this map of the modern world.

Dimetrodon, a mammal-like reptile, lived in what is now Texas during the Permian Period. The skin "sail" on its back may have served to help regulate Dimetrodon's body temperature.

most reptiles, which have no internal control over their body temperature, Dimetrodon may have used the skin "sail" on its back to help it warm up or cool down. Angling its sail face-on to the Sun would heat Dimetrodon up; adjusting the sail edge-on to the Sun would help cool it off. The mammal-like therapsids that took over during the Permian would eventually lead to the first true mammals.

The continents, moving slowly but relentlessly over Earth's surface, continued a period of mountain building that began during the Carboniferous. In Asia, for instance, such grinding collisions had created the Ural Mountains. At the close of the Permian, part of the eastern United States thrust upward and buckled into the folds of the Appalachian Mountains, the result of a collision with Africa.

THE MESOZOIC ERA

A beaked, pig-like *rhynchosaur* (top) looks on as a *nothosaur* (bottom right) chases down a quick meal in a Triassic lagoon. Four-legged nothosaurs later gave rise to flippered *plesiosaurs* (middle left).

The Age of Reptiles

The wandering continents of the Permian grew ever closer during the Triassic Period. Around 200 million years ago, all the continental plates pressed together into a single landmass, the vast supercontinent called Pangaea. The climate continued to grow warmer and drier.

Although the mammal-like reptiles ruled the world at the end of the Permian, another group was poised to dominate them in the Triassic. From one line of small, lizard-like animals would arise the *archosaurs* ("ruling reptiles"), from which all crocodiles, dinosaurs, and flying reptiles developed. Early archosaurs included forms that looked and acted much like modern crocodiles. In fact, crocodiles are the only surviving archosaurs today.

Plateosaurus ("flat reptile"), the most common early dinosaur scientists know of, appeared late in the Triassic. About twenty-six feet (eight meters) long, it walked on four legs but may have stood on its hind legs to feed on tree tops. It had a long neck, strong limbs, and broad "hands" with a long, curved thumb claw.

Protosuchus was a relative of modern crocodiles and an ancestor of the dinosaurs. Its powerful, flattened tail helped it prey on other animals in Triassic swamps.

By the end of the Triassic, when the Pangaea supercontinent began breaking up, the archosaurs had given rise to all kinds of insect-eating, meat-eating, and plant-eating dinosaurs. One early meat-eating dinosaur found in New Mexico and Massachusetts was *Coelophysis.* Able to walk on either two or four legs, it had a long neck and tail and grew to about ten feet (three meters). It probably ate small lizards. One of the most common plant-eaters was *Plateosaurus,* which roamed Triassic lagoons in what is now northern Europe.

The skull of *Camarasaurus* reveals its small head and long, blunt teeth. This sauropod roamed the western United States in Late Jurassic times.

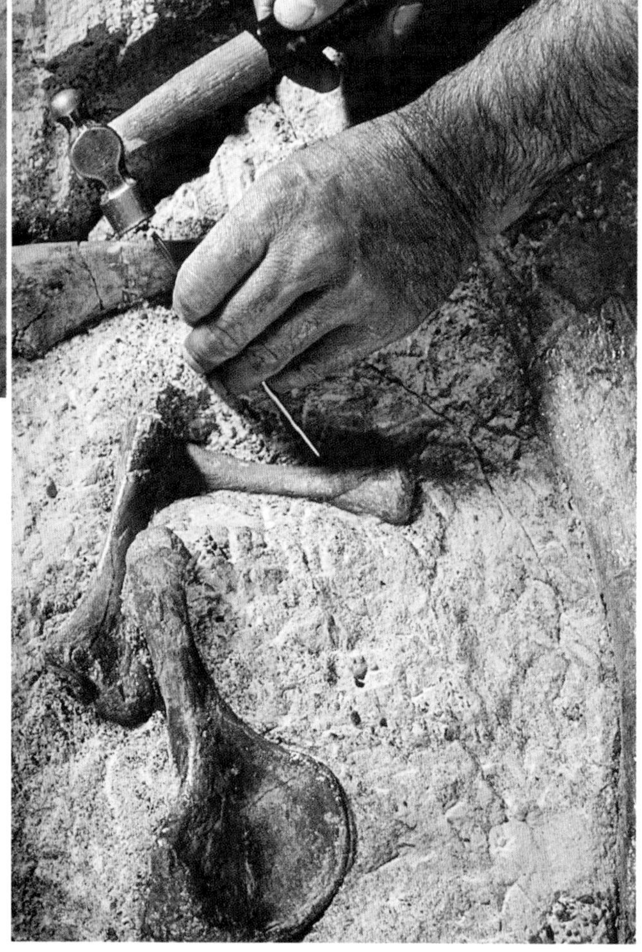

It takes time and care to separate fossil dinosaur bones from the rock that protected them for millions of years.

By the opening of the Jurassic Period 190 million years ago, reptiles flourished on the land, in the sea, and in the air. Both the largest and the smallest of all dinosaurs lived during this time.

The largest and heaviest animals were the *sauropods,* gentle plant-eaters that walked on four legs. Their huge bodies tapered into long, thin necks and tails. *Diplodocus,* the heavier *Apatosaurus* (better known as *Brontosaurus),* and the taller *Brachiosaurus* all stretched more than seventy feet (twenty-one meters) from head to tail.

Evidence of two even larger sauropods appeared in the 1970s. They lack official names, but from their apparent sizes the nicknames Supersaurus and Ultrasaurus seem appropriate. They could both easily peer over the roof of a five-story building.

In the seas, sleek fish-like *ichthyosaurs* (up to thirty-three feet or ten meters long) competed with the slower *plesiosaurs.* What plesiosaurs lacked in speed they made up for in length, with long-necked varieties reaching forty feet (twelve meters).

Reptiles took to the Jurassic skies. By the Late Triassic, some lizard-like reptiles had developed an extendable web of skin that let them glide between trees. From these gliding lizards arose the Jurassic *pterosaurs* ("winged reptiles").

Pterosaurs first appeared about 200 million years ago. Among the more than eighty species known were insect-eaters no larger than modern birds and giant scavengers that were the largest animals ever to take to the air. At least some pterosaurs even had fur.

About 150 million years ago, a new creation took flight. The crow-sized animal had a beak, sharp teeth, claws extending from the wings, and feathers. *Archaeopteryx* ("ancient wing") is the first recorded bird.

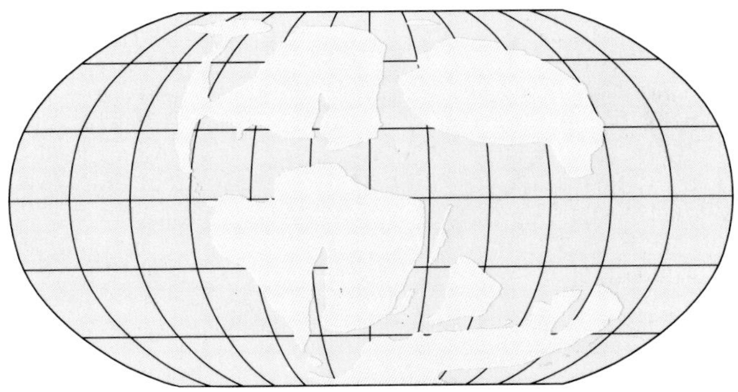

Pangaea had begun to rift apart by the end of the Late Jurassic, about 135 million years ago.

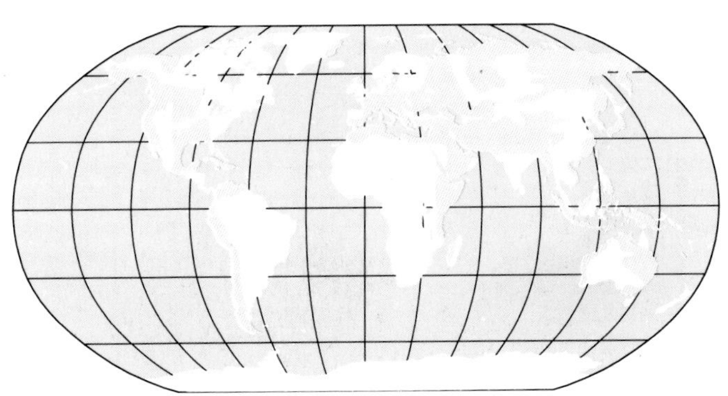

Rocks containing fossils from the Triassic and Jurassic are common in Africa, Asia, Australia, Europe, and the Americas.

The sauropods were the largest and heaviest reptiles that ever lived. Two recent discoveries, nicknamed Supersaurus and Ultrasaurus, grazed in what is now Colorado in Late Jurassic times. The forelegs alone of Ultrasaurus would be as tall as a modern giraffe.

Supersaurus

Ultrasaurus

Brachiosaurus

Human

Twilight of the Dinosaurs

During the Cretaceous Period, between 135 and 65 million years ago, South America began rifting from Africa. The Atlantic Ocean opened and widened, the climate cooled, and the dinosaur population became its most numerous and diverse.

The cooler weather helped make a revolution in plant life more widespread. Flowering plants appeared in the Cretaceous. These plants protected their seeds within a special casing, called a *fruit*, and they included all flowers, grasses, and most of the agricultural products we grow today. Magnolias were one of the earliest flowering plants to bloom. Such modern trees as the oak, aspen, and poplar developed, too.

The earlier Mesozoic experiments with flying animals proved successful. True birds, the descendants of *Archaeopteryx*, developed throughout the Cretaceous. The flying reptiles grew their largest. The *Pteranodon*, sporting wings over twenty-four feet (seven me-

Flowering plants appeared during the Cretaceous Period, and magnolias (left) were among the first to bloom. Modern trees, such as the oak (center) and aspen (right), also made appearances.

Following the scent of the rotting carcass, several giant pterosaurs circle a dead *Alamosaurus.* The largest animal ever to fly, the wings of Quetzalcoatlus stretched nearly forty-three feet (twelve meters) from tip to tip.

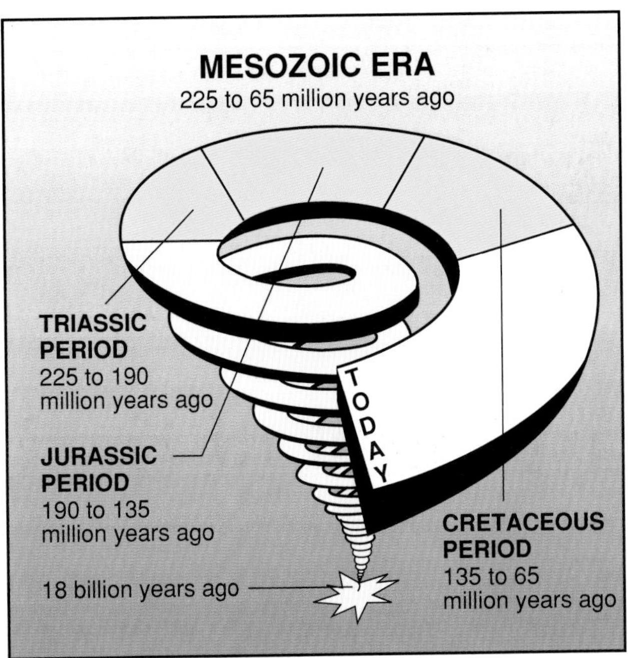

Reptiles dominated the world during the Mesozoic Era, between 225 million and 65 million years ago.

ters) across, launched itself into the wind from cliffside roosts and skimmed the sea in search of fish.

Until the 1970s, Pteranodons were believed to be the largest of the flying reptiles. Then Texas scientists unearthed *Quetzalcoatlus,* a giant pterosaur scavenger whose wings stretched over forty-three feet (twelve meters)—the largest creature ever to take wing.

Among the least-threatening dinosaurs ever were the *hadrosaurs.* They were also known as duck-billed dinosaurs for their broad, flat, toothless snouts. They walked about on two legs, nibbling on plants growing at the edges of freshwater ponds.

The Cretaceous Period was host to quite a variety of tank-sized, heavily armored plant-eaters. *Stegosaurus,* for example, had rows of bony plates along its back and long bony spikes on the end of its tail. The plates may have been used for more than defense. Some scientists believe that the plates helped regulate the animal's body temperature—the same technique theoretically used by Dimetrodon during the Permian.

Another well-armed group was the *ceratopsians* (''horned faces''). Animals like *Torosaurus, Triceratops,* and *Styracosaurus* were protected by horny spikes on their faces and a bony frill around the head. The frill of Torosaurus was the largest of all, making the animal's skull up to 8.5 feet (2.6 meters) long.

With the powerful carnivores that roamed the Cretaceous world, such elaborate defenses were necessary. A quick drink from a lake or river could turn deadly as *Phobosuchus,* the fifty-foot-long (fifteen meters) ''horror crocodile,'' lashed out for a meal. It was the biggest crocodile that ever lived.

Corythosaurus is one of the largest and best known hadrosaurs, also called duck-billed dinosaurs because of their toothless beaks. Over thirty-three feet (ten meters) long, Corythosaurus had a high, narrow crest atop its head.

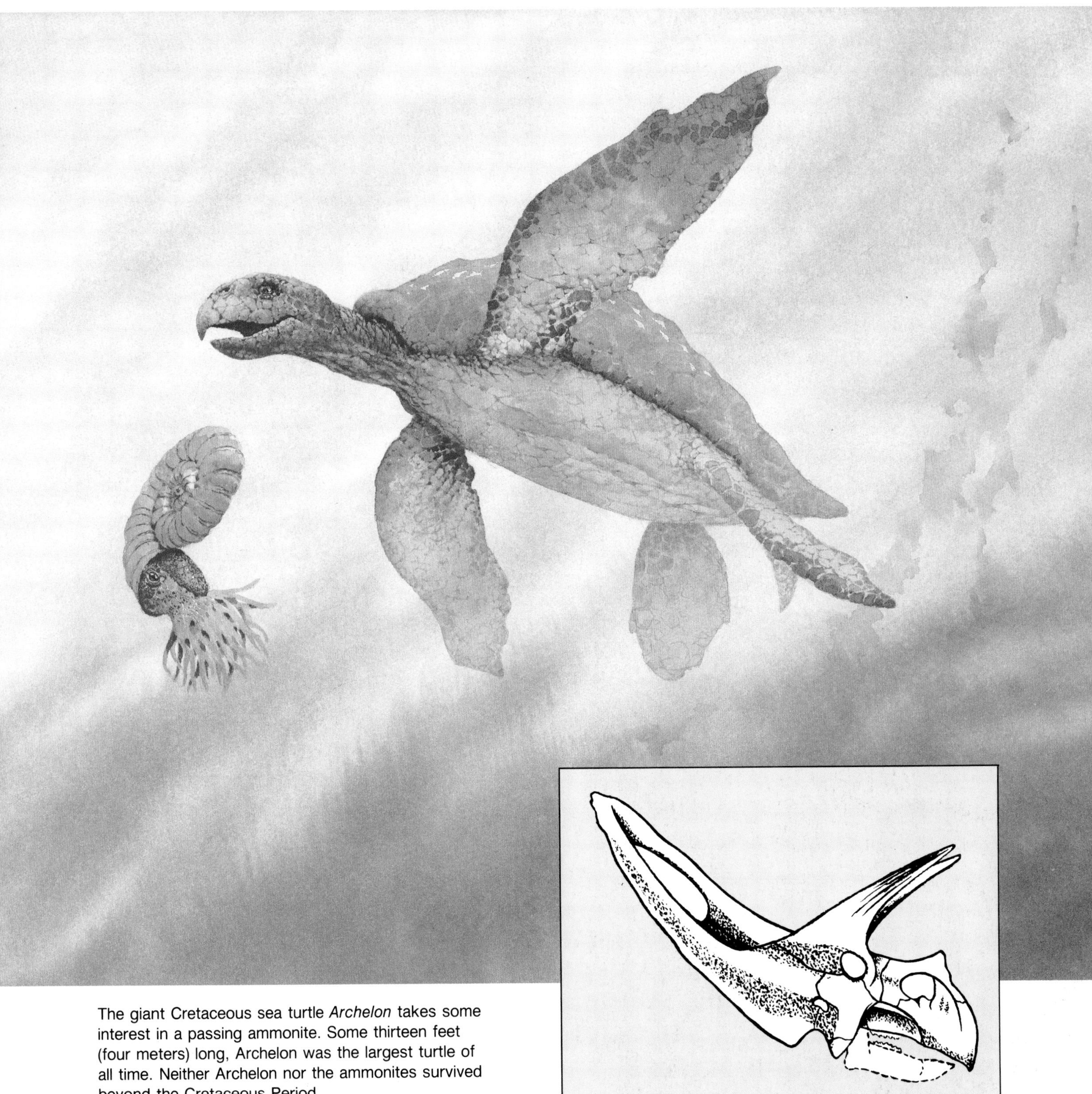

The giant Cretaceous sea turtle *Archelon* takes some interest in a passing ammonite. Some thirteen feet (four meters) long, Archelon was the largest turtle of all time. Neither Archelon nor the ammonites survived beyond the Cretaceous Period.

Torosaurus was a three-horned plant-eater related to the more familiar Triceratops. Its skull, backed by an elaborate frill, gave Torosaurus the largest head of any known land animal. Shown here is a drawing of a Torosaurus fossil skull. The dotted line shows what the missing jaw bone probably looks like.

Tyrannosaurus (at right) was the most fearsome killer of its time. Up to fifty feet (fifteen meters) long, it held its huge head twenty feet (six meters) above the ground. Triceratops (below) normally kept far from meat-eaters. If cornered, though, its head frill and horns gave Triceratops a fighting chance.

The Cretaceous Period saw the development of the most frightening predator dinosaur of all: *Tyrannosaurus.* This monster is probably the best known dinosaur. Its powerful jaws were lined with seven-inch-long (eighteen centimeters) teeth. It stood on two muscular legs but walked with its head lowered and thrust forward. If one were around today, it could probably swallow a human whole. No matter how well armed the plant-eaters were, none of them were anxious to tangle with Tyrannosaurus.

Triceratops, the last and largest of the ceratopsians, was a brute in its own right. The animal grew up to thirty-six feet (eleven meters) long. The two long horns above its eyes could be up to three feet (one meter) long. Even a very determined tyrannosaur would get out of the way of a charging Triceratops. Still, there must have been battles. Some Triceratops fossils show where wounds on the bony frills or horns had healed.

Smaller meat-eaters could be just as deadly as tyrannosaurs. Six-foot-long (1.8 meters) *Velociraptor* ("swift robber"), for example, raced after its prey and raked its victims with a huge, curved toe claw. A fossil discovered in 1971 gave scientists an unusual glimpse of a Velociraptor's attack on a *Protoceratops.*

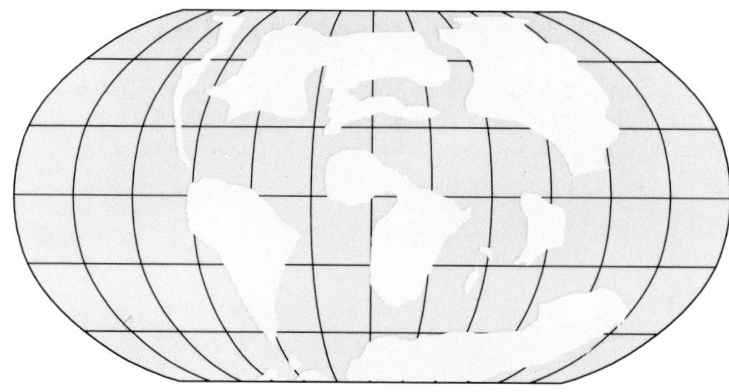

South America separated from Africa during the Cretaceous Period, widening the Atlantic Ocean. This is the way the world looked about sixty-five million years ago.

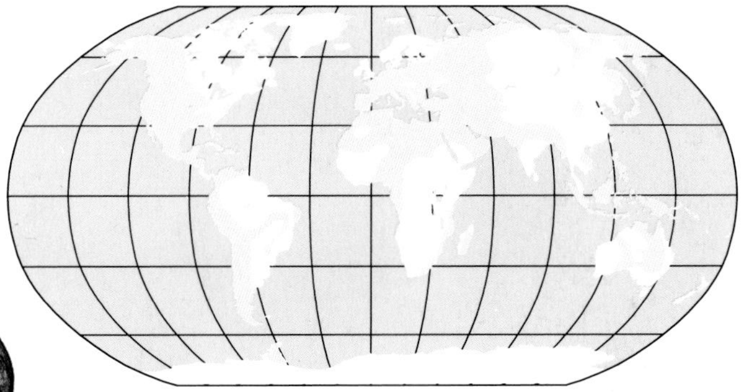

This scene was frozen into a fossil found in 1971. The beak of a Protoceratops had pierced the chest of an attacking Velociraptor, but the meat-eater's foot claw had slashed the belly of its prey. They must have died at the same time.

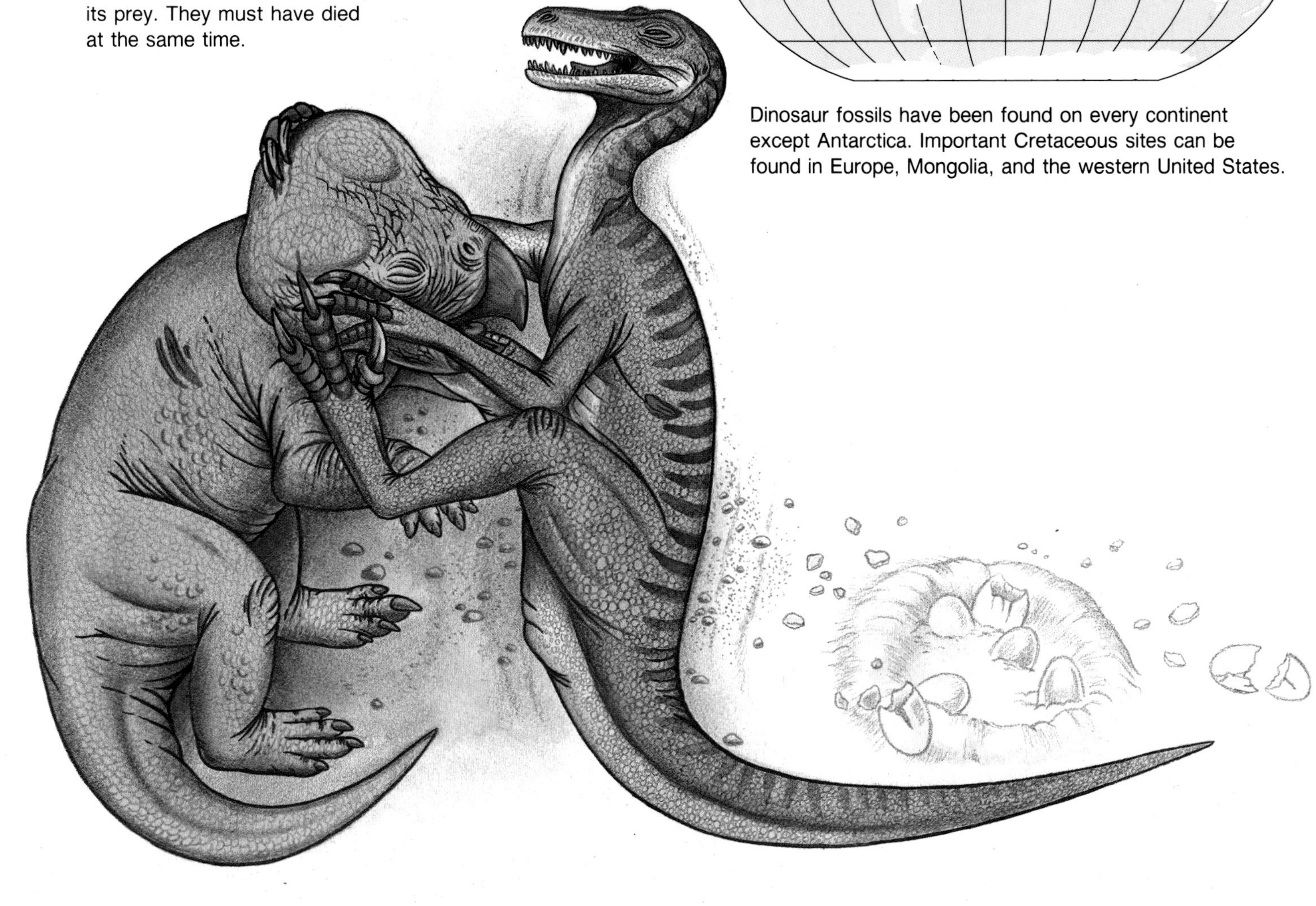

Dinosaur fossils have been found on every continent except Antarctica. Important Cretaceous sites can be found in Europe, Mongolia, and the western United States.

Dinosaurs, pterosaurs, aquatic reptiles, and many plants died off at the end of the Cretaceous Period. The great extinction provided new opportunities for the small, shrew-like mammals that had been around since the Jurassic.

The Great Extinction

Dinosaurs ruled the Earth for 140 million years, but they disappear from the fossil record 65 million years ago. What killed off the dinosaurs has been the subject of wild speculation for decades. Everything from exploding stars to indigestion has been proposed to explain it.

Most of these ideas focus too much on the dinosaurs. In fact, many other groups vanished as the Cretaceous closed. That amazing group of flying reptiles, the pterosaurs, were wiped out completely. The sea-going reptiles—ichthyosaurs, plesiosaurs, and others—vanished from the oceans. Ammonites and belemnites swam in the ancient seas eons before dinosaurs, and they too disappeared. Many have wondered why.

In 1980, a group of scientists studying the clay layer formed at the end of the Cretaceous announced something unusual. The clay con-

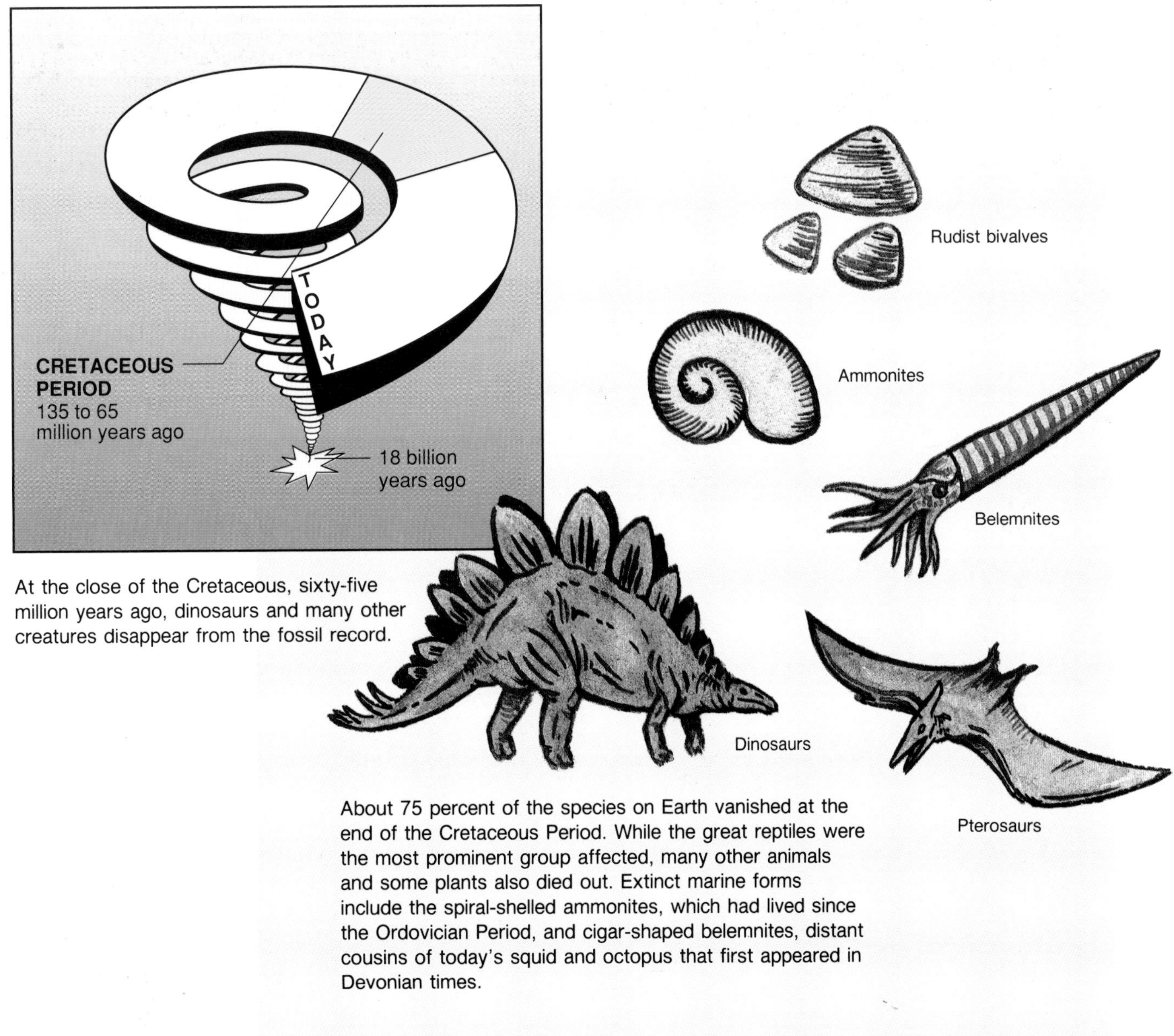

At the close of the Cretaceous, sixty-five million years ago, dinosaurs and many other creatures disappear from the fossil record.

About 75 percent of the species on Earth vanished at the end of the Cretaceous Period. While the great reptiles were the most prominent group affected, many other animals and some plants also died out. Extinct marine forms include the spiral-shelled ammonites, which had lived since the Ordovician Period, and cigar-shaped belemnites, distant cousins of today's squid and octopus that first appeared in Devonian times.

tained the element iridium at levels 160 times higher than normal. The element is rare in Earth's crust but is common in meteorites. Taking the total amount of iridium into account, the scientists suggested that the Earth was struck by a giant meteorite about six miles (ten kilometers) across. The effects of this tremendous impact, they argued, resulted in the Cretaceous mass extinction.

Geologists originally resisted the idea, apparently believing that such violent collisions were extremely rare in Earth's history. Astronomers countered with evidence based on studies of the Moon's craters. On average, they said, Earth is struck by objects of about the right size every ten million years. In addition, geologists since have found in the clay deformed ("shocked") quartz crystals and tiny glass spheres—the expected by-products of a giant meteorite impact.

Evidence of past collisions with asteroids and comets lies within more than 100 impact craters scientists have identified on the Earth. Shown here is the peaceful Earth before an impact.

Streaking through the atmosphere at thirty times the speed of sound, a half-mile-wide (0.8 kilometer) asteroid is immediately surrounded by a glowing sheath of superheated air.

Today, most geologists accept the evidence that a large asteroid or comet slammed into the Earth sixty-five million years ago. The atmosphere usually stops small meteorites, but the Cretaceous asteroid would have plunged through unaffected. Striking the Earth's crust with the force of millions upon millions of tons of TNT, the asteroid gouged out a crater some 62 miles (100 kilometers) across and was instantly turned to vapor. The crater cannot be found today, probably because it struck the ocean floor and was slowly erased by the moving continents.

A brilliant fireball expanded from the site of impact, setting great forest fires. Shock waves rebounding through the crust blasted a plume of dust and rock high into the atmosphere. Spreading around the globe, the dust blocked sunlight and plunged Earth into months of darkness. Plants died off. This killed the plant-eating animals that meat-eaters hunted. Acid rains may have polluted the seas, weakening the shells of many marine forms.

Other mass extinctions pepper the fossil record, as the table at right shows. The one that ended the Permian Period was even more devastating than the one that closed the Cretaceous. Some scientists feel that it too was caused by an impact, but there is no firm evidence.

Lake Manicouagan in Quebec, Canada, fills the ring-shaped scar of an impact crater hollowed out 210 million years ago by a giant meteorite.

Slamming into the Earth with the force of a million tons of TNT, the meteorite splashes into an ancient sea and blasts tons of water, rock, and dust high into the atmosphere.

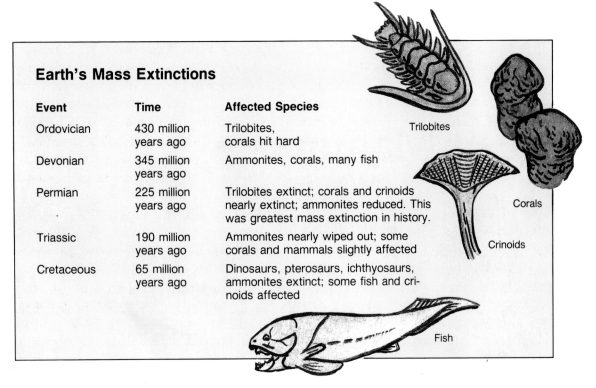

Earth's Mass Extinctions

Event	Time	Affected Species
Ordovician	430 million years ago	Trilobites, corals hit hard
Devonian	345 million years ago	Ammonites, corals, many fish
Permian	225 million years ago	Trilobites extinct; corals and crinoids nearly extinct; ammonites reduced. This was greatest mass extinction in history.
Triassic	190 million years ago	Ammonites nearly wiped out; some corals and mammals slightly affected
Cretaceous	65 million years ago	Dinosaurs, pterosaurs, ichthyosaurs, ammonites extinct; some fish and crinoids affected

THE CENOZOIC ERA

The Age of Mammals

Mammals had changed little since the arrival of the dinosaurs. Throughout the 140-million-year reign of the giant reptiles, mammals remained no larger than mice. The rapid development of reptiles into every habitat on Earth may have kept the tiny mammals scurrying. There was simply no opportunity for development.

When opportunity came, however, the mammals were ready. Within ten million years after the extinction of the dinosaurs, mammals of every size and life-style appeared. Rodents, whales, early horses, pigs, bats, meat-eaters and plant-eaters—they were all present.

One key to the success of mammals was a revolution in the way they bore their young. Instead of laying eggs like most of the reptiles, the ancient mammals began bearing live young. Born at a very early stage of develop-

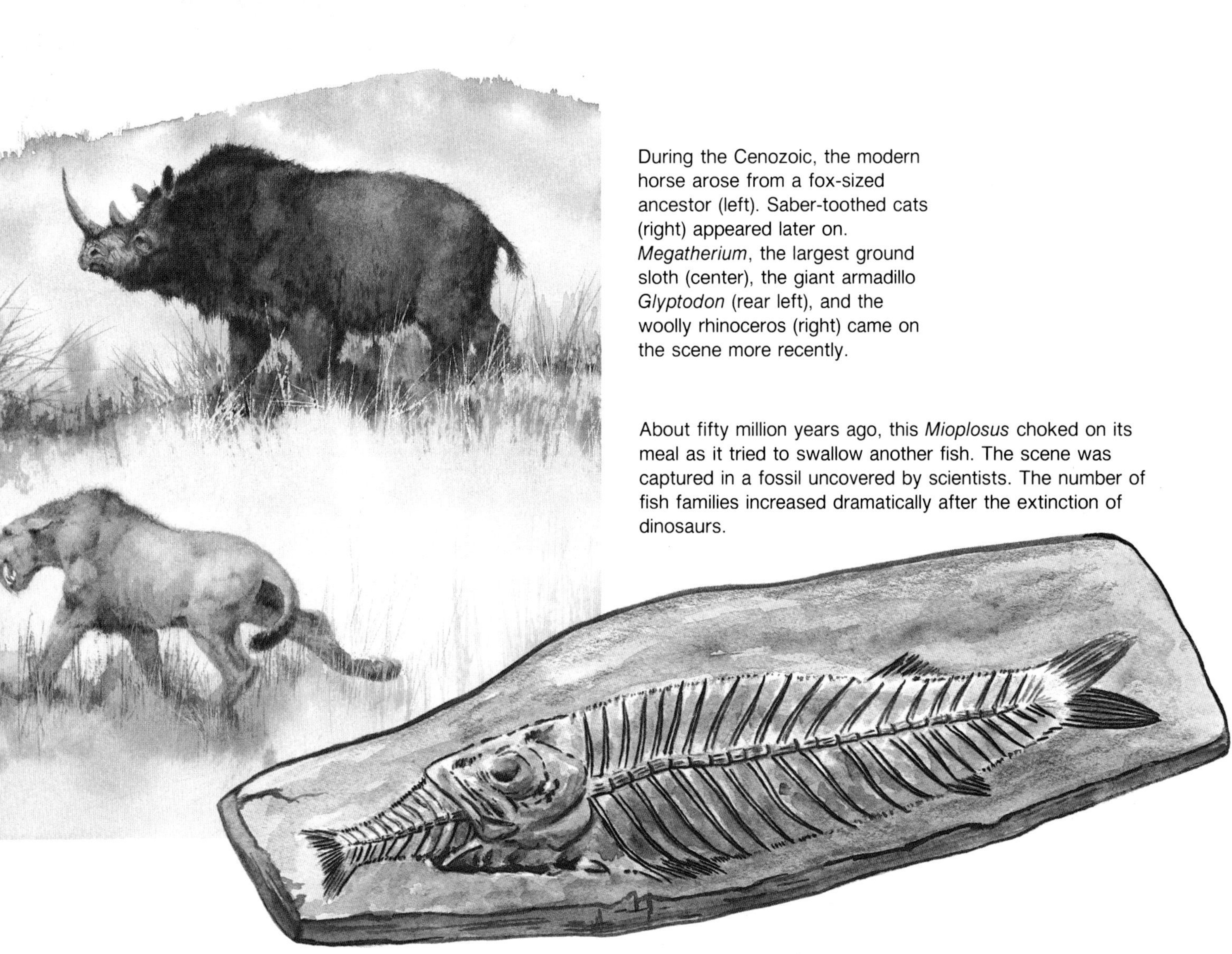

During the Cenozoic, the modern horse arose from a fox-sized ancestor (left). Saber-toothed cats (right) appeared later on. *Megatherium*, the largest ground sloth (center), the giant armadillo *Glyptodon* (rear left), and the woolly rhinoceros (right) came on the scene more recently.

About fifty million years ago, this *Mioplosus* choked on its meal as it tried to swallow another fish. The scene was captured in a fossil uncovered by scientists. The number of fish families increased dramatically after the extinction of dinosaurs.

ment, the young were transferred to a pouch on the mother's belly and nourished with their mother's milk. They stayed in the pouch until they were large enough to fend for themselves. These were the first *marsupials;* modern versions include the kangaroo and opossum.

Marsupials flourished in South America, Australia, and probably Antarctica. The three continents separated during the Cretaceous Period, isolating their marsupial mammals. As soon as the dinosaurs died out the marsupials took off. This was especially true in Australia, where they occupied every habitat available.

Northern mammals did things a little differently. They held their young within their bodies in an internal "pouch." Nutrients and oxygen were passed from the mother's blood directly to the unborn young.

Standing eighteen feet (5.5 meters) high, *Baluchitherium* could easily nibble twigs and leaves. Baluchitherium was the world's biggest rhinoceros and the largest land mammal that ever lived.

Most modern mammals—including humans—reproduce by the method of these later mammals. Ancestors of modern mammals, the mammals of the early Tertiary were smart, quick insect-eaters ready to inherit the Earth.

But it would not be easy. Birds had also survived the Cretaceous extinction, and about 40 million years ago a new type of meat-eating bird appeared in Antarctica and South America. They were the *phororhacids.* About six feet (two meters) tall, these large-beaked, short-necked, flightless birds dominated their lands. They were the only large running predators for millions of years. Chasing down a marsupial meal, these birds probably held their prey with one taloned foot and tore it apart with their beaks.

Similar predatory birds developed in Europe and North America. One, called *Diatryma,* lived in Wyoming about thirty million years ago. These birds were not as successful as their distant relatives in South America. There probably was competition for dominance between these giant birds and the mammals of the day. Eventually, the mammals emerged victorious, but the contest could have gone the other way.

About five million years ago, volcanoes between North and South America began building up the Isthmus of Panama. As the land bridge formed, the meat-eating mammals of the north invaded. They wiped out all but a few of the South American marsupials, and today only the opossum survives. The climate turned cooler and drier as Antarctica slid toward its present position and began icing over, and the phororhacids and their relatives slowly died off.

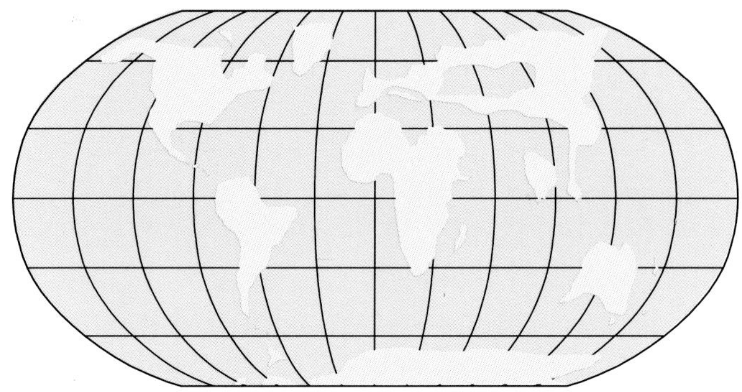

During the Tertiary Period, between 65 and 1.8 million years ago, the continents approached their present positions. Shown here is the world about 35 million years ago.

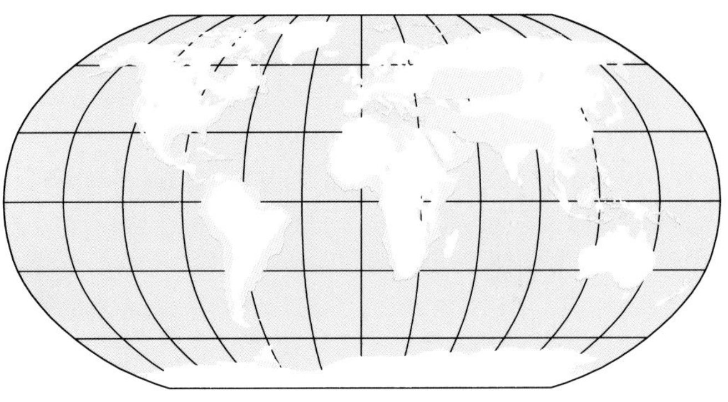

Early Cenozoic deposits are tinted in this map of the modern world.

Birds and mammals were rivals in the Tertiary Period. In South America and Antarctica, the largest meat-eaters were a group of flightless birds called phororhacids. The terror of small grazing mammals, the six-foot-tall birds disappeared about three million years ago. A North American relative, Diatryma, was not as successful.

Advance of the Glaciers

The cooling climate of the Tertiary Period turned into the great Ice Ages of the Quaternary Period. Between about 1.8 million and ten thousand years ago, a period called the Pleistocene Epoch, glaciers and vast ice sheets made four or five major advances across the continents.

No one knows exactly what caused the great Ice Ages, but it is certain that slight variations in the Earth's yearly orbit around the Sun contributed to them. The glaciers surged forward, retreated as the climate warmed, then advanced again when the cold returned. At the height of the last Ice Age twenty thousand years ago, vast ice sheets more than two miles (3.2 kilometers) thick stretched as far south as Europe and the midwestern United States. So much water was locked up in the ice that world sea levels dropped by 350 feet (106 meters).

During the cool periods, heavy snows fell in the polar regions. Gradually, as the snow deepened to about one hundred feet (thirty meters), its sheer weight turned the bottom layers to ice. Sluggishly, the ice sheet, or *glacier,* began moving downhill. Boulders frozen into its bottom layer raked across the landscape, grinding, polishing, and scratching the rock over which the ice moved.

TODAY

QUATERNARY PERIOD
1.8 million years ago to present

18 billion years ago

Pleistocene Epoch
1.8 million to 10,000 years ago

Giant sheets of ice made several advances across the Quaternary landscape between 1.8 million and ten thousand years ago.

In places where the ice was thickest, Earth's crust is still reacting to the last ice sheet, even though it melted away some ten thousand years ago. Near the shores of Lake Superior in North America, the land is rising by about fifteen inches (thirty-eight centimeters) per century, slowly rebounding from the ice sheet's crushing weight.

Many scientists believe that human civilization is now enjoying the warm period between two ice ages. Thousands of years from now, the ice may return.

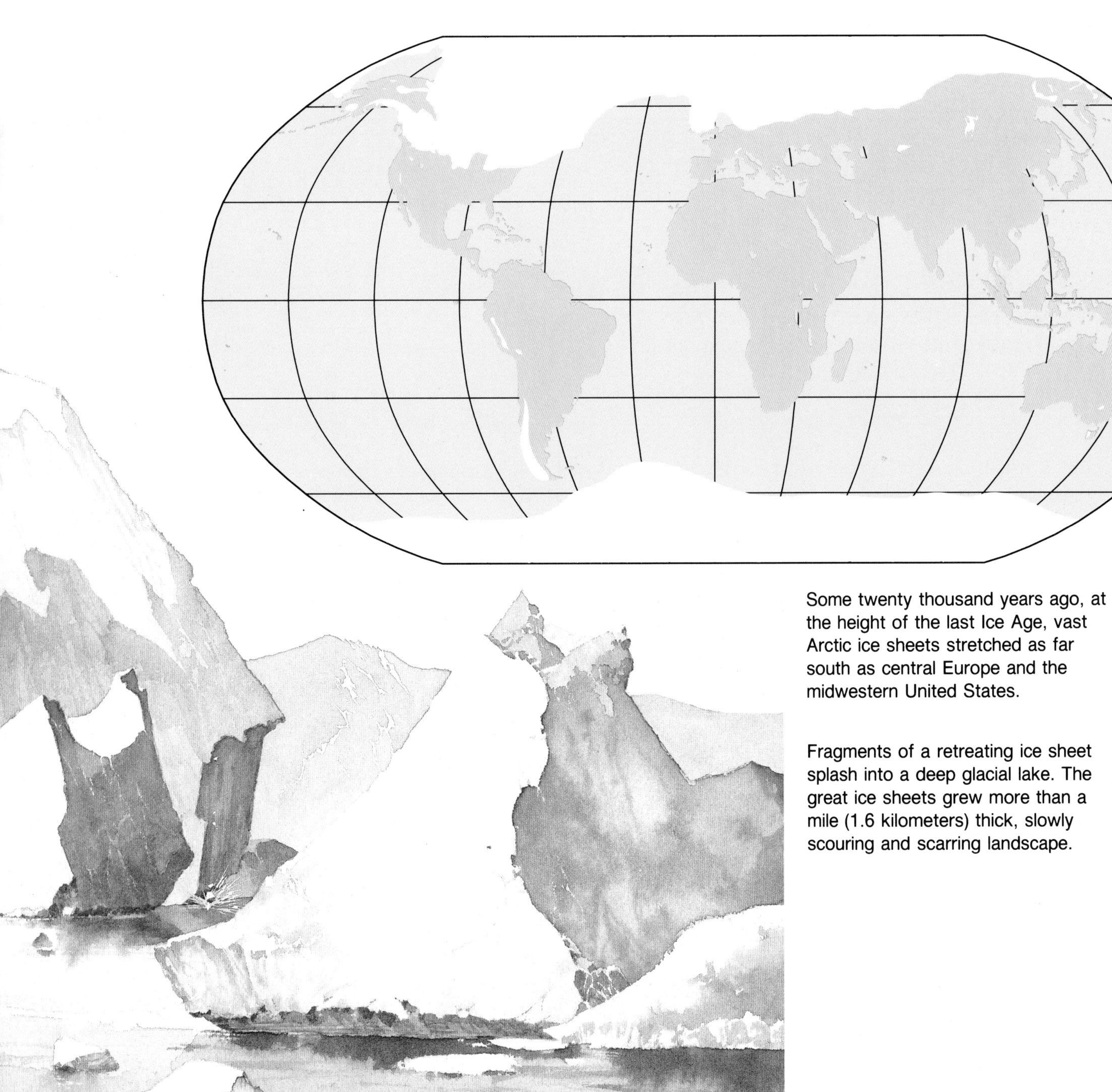

Some twenty thousand years ago, at the height of the last Ice Age, vast Arctic ice sheets stretched as far south as central Europe and the midwestern United States.

Fragments of a retreating ice sheet splash into a deep glacial lake. The great ice sheets grew more than a mile (1.6 kilometers) thick, slowly scouring and scarring landscape.

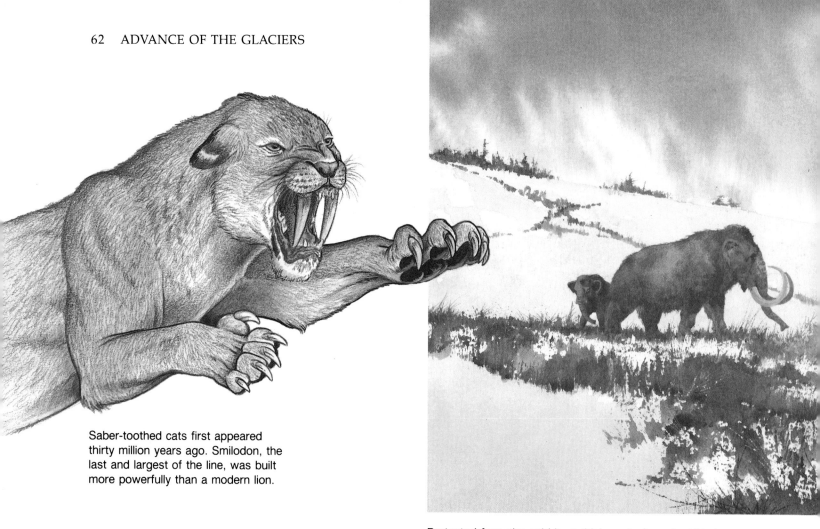

Saber-toothed cats first appeared thirty million years ago. Smilodon, the last and largest of the line, was built more powerfully than a modern lion.

Protected from the cold by a thick coat of wool and hair, herds of mammoth roamed Europe, Asia, and North America. Up to thirteen feet (four meters) high at the shoulder, they were slightly larger than modern elephants.

The mammals that exploded onto the scene during the Tertiary developed into some strange forms during the Pleistocene Epoch. Teeth and bones locked within sediments of this time are easy to recover. About 85 percent of the mammal species now living in Europe are represented as fossils within Pleistocene sediments.

A rich source of fossils from this time are the solidified asphalt pools known as tar pits. Animals stumbling into the thick, black liquid would become trapped and sink into the pool. Once solidified, the tar protected the jumbled bones of its various victims.

Saber-toothed cats first appeared early in the Tertiary Period, about thirty million years ago. They survived into the Pleistocene, where the group's largest member, *Smilodon,* ended the line. Larger and more powerful than a modern lion, Smilodon featured two enormously overgrown teeth. Smilodon was not built for running, so it probably waited in ambush for its prey. Stabbing its victim with the sharp extra-long teeth, Smilodon could rip through the thickest hides of the time. Living in North America and Europe, Smilodon probably fed on large plant-eaters. As the animals it fed upon died off, so did the last of the saber-toothed cats.

Stumbling into a thick pool of asphalt, a mammoth desperately struggles to free itself. Predators looking for an easy meal may become trapped themselves. Tar pits such as those found in the La Brea area of Southern California are a rich source of Ice Age fossils.

The ancestor of the modern horse, *Hyracotherium,* appeared as a fox-sized, North American forest dweller about fifty million years ago. By the end of the Pleistocene, its successors had developed into the modern horse. The lowered sea levels of the Ice Age resulted in a thin land bridge between Asia and North America, and horses migrated across it. Horses later died out in North America, only returning to their first home aboard the ships of European colonists.

With the onset of colder weather, many animals developed thick, hairy hides. The woolly rhinoceros, for example, roamed North America, Europe, and northern Asia. The woolly mammoth is probably the best known Ice Age mammal. Tracking through the snow-covered landscapes in great herds, the mammoth was nearly twice the weight of modern elephants. Shaggy, black hair covered its body, and great upward-curling tusks emerged from its face. It stood some thirteen feet tall (four meters) and measured nearly twenty-four feet (over seven meters) from tusk to tail.

The giant ground sloth *Megatherium* lived predominantly in South America. Up to 18 feet (5.5 meters) long, this ancestor of modern sloths walked on four legs, but reared up to full height to reach the foliage it fed upon. Another South American mammal was an ancestor of modern armadillos. Living in roughly the same geographic area as Megatherium, the giant *Glyptodon* was up to nine feet (2.7 meters) long.

The early Tertiary Period also saw the origin of early *primates,* the family to which apes, chimpanzees, and human beings belong. As Tertiary forests gave way to Pleistocene grasslands, these primates were poised for the climb toward humanity.

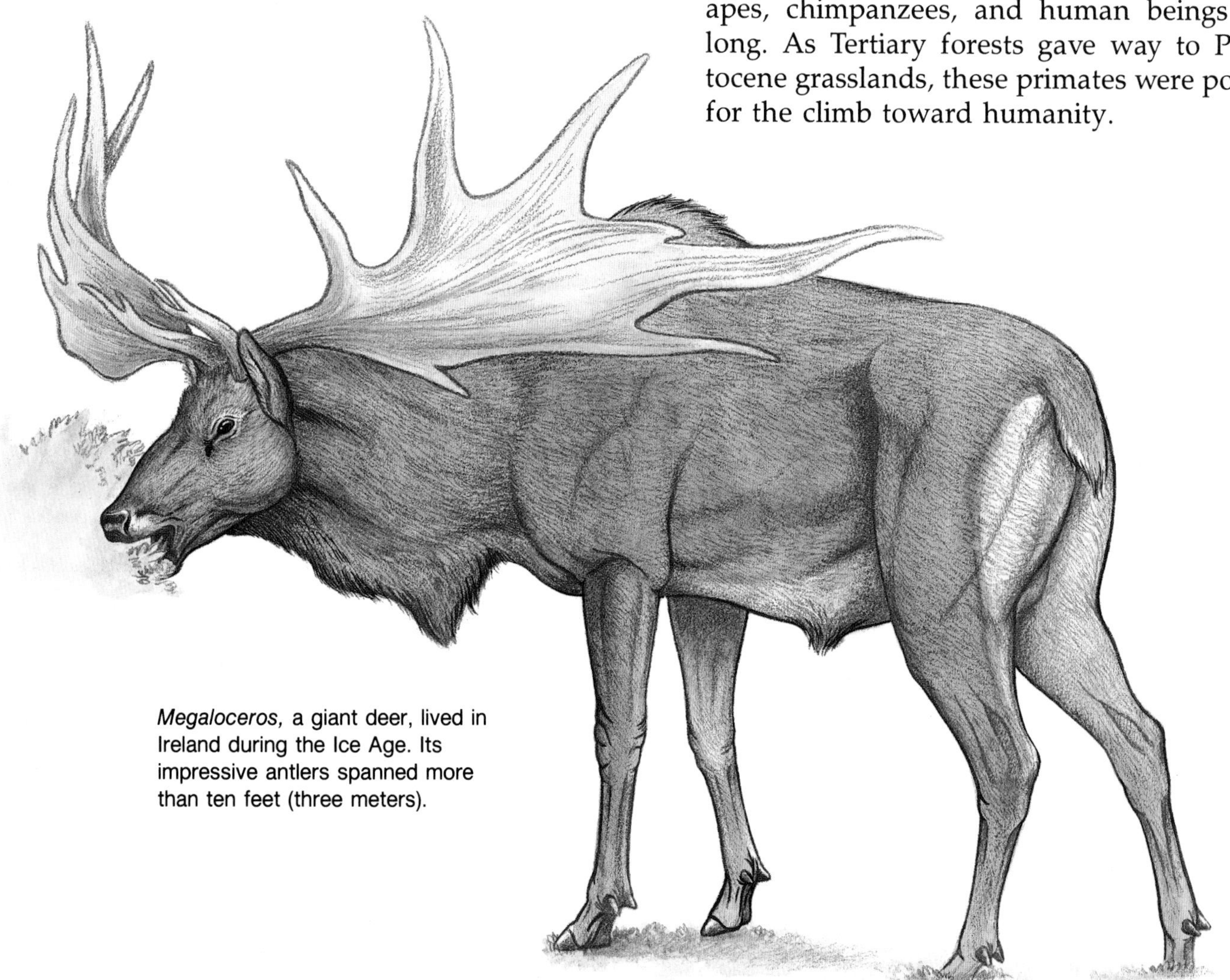

Megaloceros, a giant deer, lived in Ireland during the Ice Age. Its impressive antlers spanned more than ten feet (three meters).

Toward the end of the Tertiary Period, around three million years ago, there appeared primates that walked upright through the grasslands of eastern Africa. They represent the earliest well-established members of the human family.

A more sophisticated tool maker than *Homo habilis*, *Homo erectus* appears to have been the first to control one of the most important tools—fire. *Homo erectus* was the first to migrate into Asia and Europe.

The Coming of Humans

Early in the Tertiary Period, when mammals rapidly expanded into habitats abandoned by the dinosaurs, the number of primate-type mammals increased. By about thirty million years ago, tailed, four-legged animals about the size of a house cat danced through the trees of the dense African forest. Fossils of one such creature, named *Aegyptopithecus*, were discovered in 1961 in Egypt—a glimpse of what may be one of the oldest ancestors of apes and humans.

Here the story becomes more clouded. Only the twenty-million-year-old fossils of another tree-dwelling primate, the baboon-sized *Proconsul*, links the earlier ape-like primates to later *hominid* (human-like) apes.

As the Tertiary Period closed and the great forests gave way to grasslands, an impressive creature arose in eastern Africa. Called *Australopithecus* (southern ape), this small-bodied primate walked on two legs and lived in groups. Some 3.6 million years ago, a trio of these prehumans went for a long walk along a muddy flat. The fossilized tracks, which were found near Laetoli, Tanzania, in the late 1970s, leave no doubt about their upright posture. Standing only about four and one-half feet (about one and one-half meters) tall on average, Australopithecus remains have been found in Kenya, Ethiopia, South Africa, and Tanzania.

By the beginning of the Quaternary Period, a somewhat larger hominid had appeared. Its hand structure probably approached that of modern humans, for this primate made crude tools. The earliest stone tools were made about 1.8 million years ago. Using one rock to flake off pieces of another, *Homo habilis* fashioned the first cutting tools—and the beginnings of civilization.

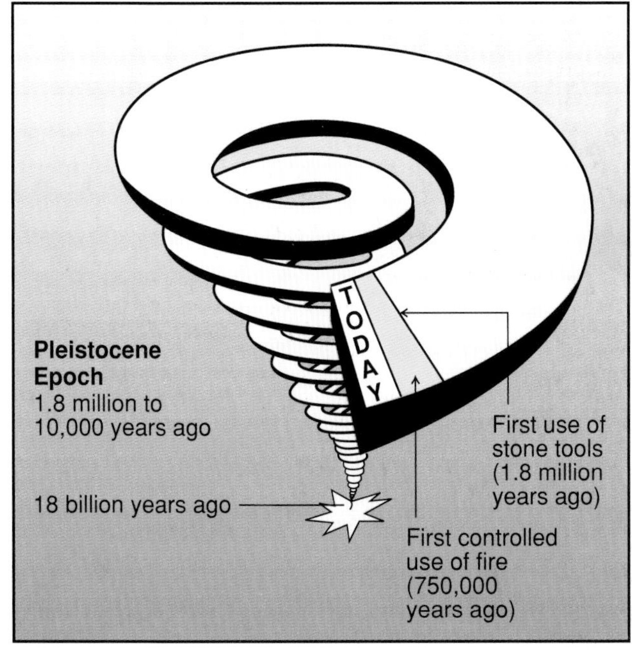

The earliest humans, *Homo habilis*, made stone tools in the grasslands of Africa some 1.8 millon years ago. Their successors, *Homo erectus*, learned how to control fire about 750,000 years ago.

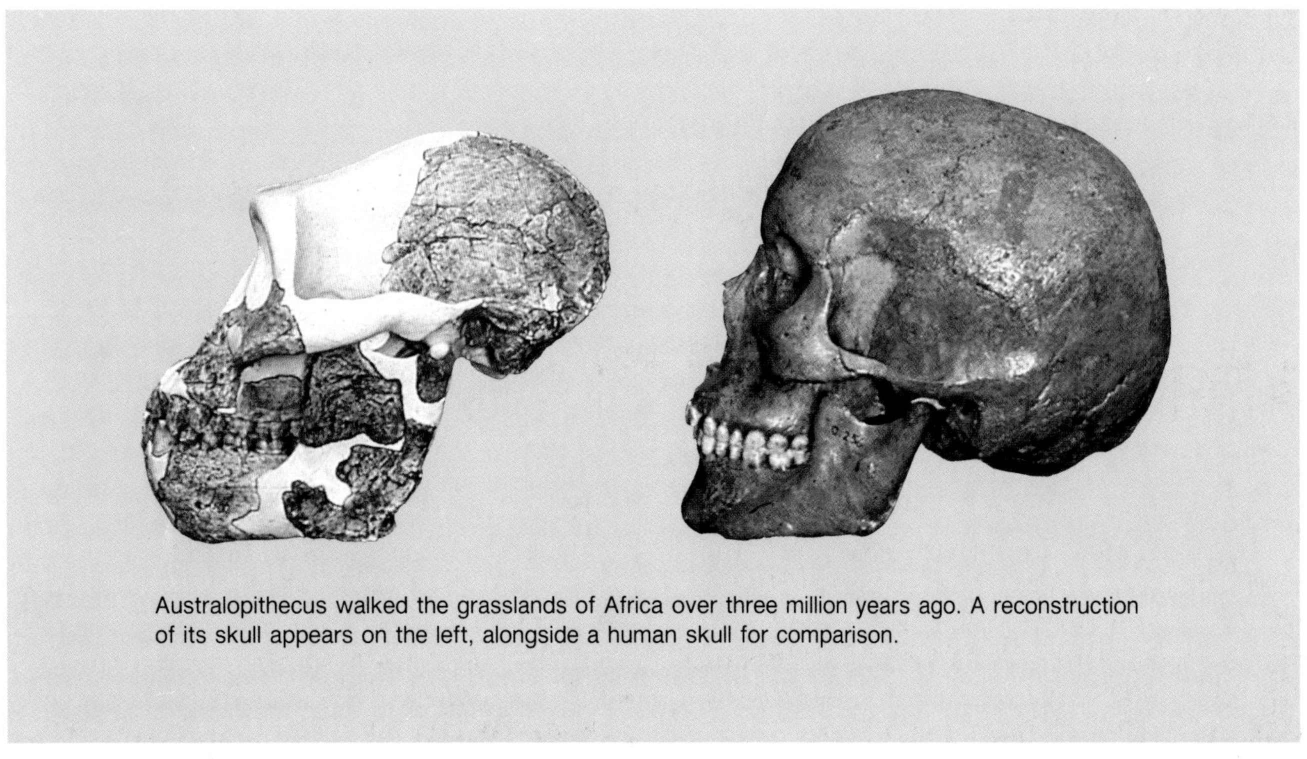

Australopithecus walked the grasslands of Africa over three million years ago. A reconstruction of its skull appears on the left, alongside a human skull for comparison.

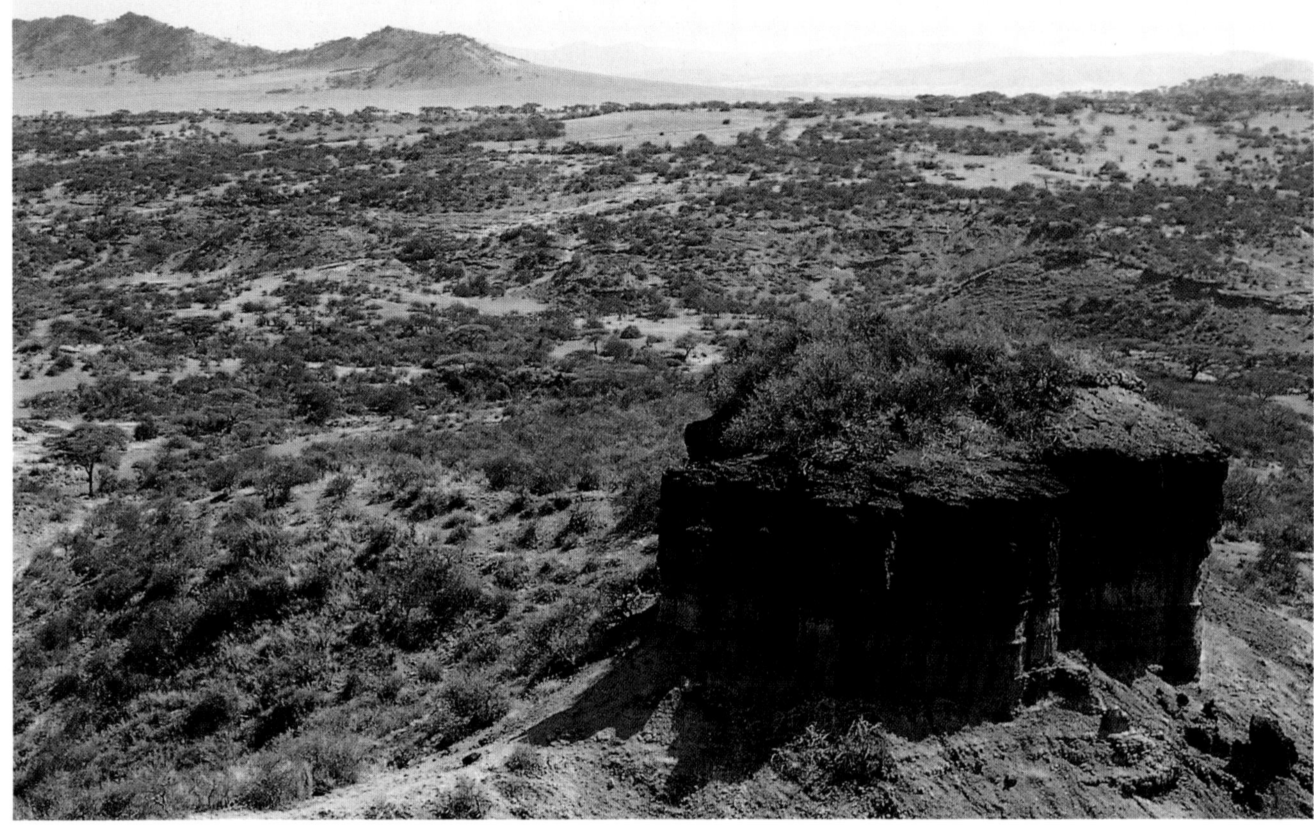

Although this photograph of Olduvai Gorge today shows a sun-baked plain, this was the site of an ancient lake. Human ancestors lived along the shores of the lake. Remains of their settlements—and fossilized bones of the creatures themselves—have been discovered in the gorge.

Another hominid appeared on the scene about 1.5 million years ago—*Homo erectus*. Slightly smaller than modern humans, Homo erectus is responsible for several innovations. About one million years ago, bands of Homo erectus became the first to leave Africa, the ancestral home of the hominid family, and moved into Europe and Asia. No one knows why hominids began the migration out of Africa, or why it took so long for them to venture forth.

Scientists also credit this group with one of civilization's most important advances—the control of fire. The earliest evidence comes from a cave in France, where charcoal, ash, and fire-cracked stone show where hearths burned some 750,000 years ago. Homo erectus also made improved stone tools.

About 300,000 years ago, the immediate ancestors of modern humans began their emergence. Nicknamed Neanderthal Man, they are more precisely known as *Homo sapiens neanderthalensis*. Their large heads often held a brain bigger than that of modern humans. Their foreheads were sloped, and bony ridges arched over their eyes. Neanderthals were the first hominids to bury their dead, and many sites suggest that, like today, burials were important ceremonies.

By about 40,000 years ago, a new breed of human—nicknamed Cro-Magnon Man—displaced the Neanderthals. Just how this happened is not at all clear, but an early suggestion that the Cro-Magnons killed off their older relatives is no longer seriously considered. They were *Homo sapiens sapiens*, the scientific name for modern humans. They created sophisticated tools for hunting, jewelry from shells and ivory, and magnificent multicolored cave paintings.

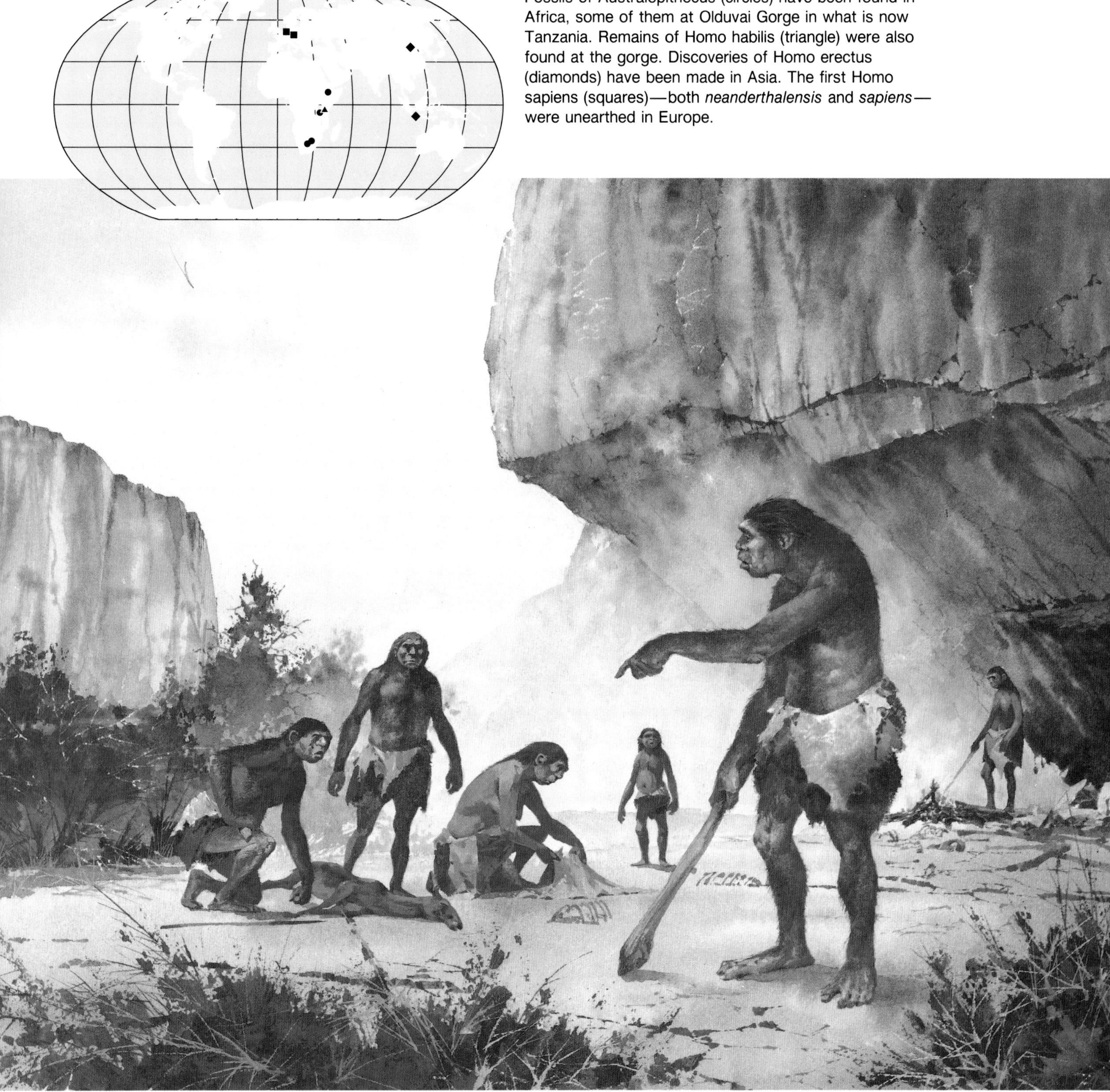

Fossils of Australopithecus (circles) have been found in Africa, some of them at Olduvai Gorge in what is now Tanzania. Remains of Homo habilis (triangle) were also found at the gorge. Discoveries of Homo erectus (diamonds) have been made in Asia. The first Homo sapiens (squares)—both *neanderthalensis* and *sapiens*—were unearthed in Europe.

Cro-Magnon cave dwellers of the last Ice Age decorated their homes with colorful works of art. They painted with fingers, sticks, pads of fur, and even developed spray-painting by blowing through hollow, paint-filled bones.

The Sun rises over the steel-and-glass skyscrapers of Chicago, a symbol of humanity's incredible progress. In terms of the vast span of geologic time, the rise from cave-dweller to cosmopolitan has been explosive.

What's in Store for Us?

Between the prehistoric cave art of the Cro-Magnon and the bustling cities of modern times lie the great civilizations of history—among them, Sumeria and Babylon, Greece and Rome. When one considers the vast abyss of geologic time, the rise of humanity has occurred with unbelievable speed—literally the blink of the eye.

Our Pleistocene ancestors endured winters far more severe than anything modern humans have ever experienced. At a time when thick ice sheets covered much of Europe and Asia, humans were devising tools, creating art, banding together in communities of increasing size and complexity.

Near the close of the Pleistocene, a few groups wandered across a bridge of land that connected Asia with North America, opening a vast new area for human expansion. In only a few thousand years, people spread all the way to the tip of South America.

When the glaciers retreated and the sea

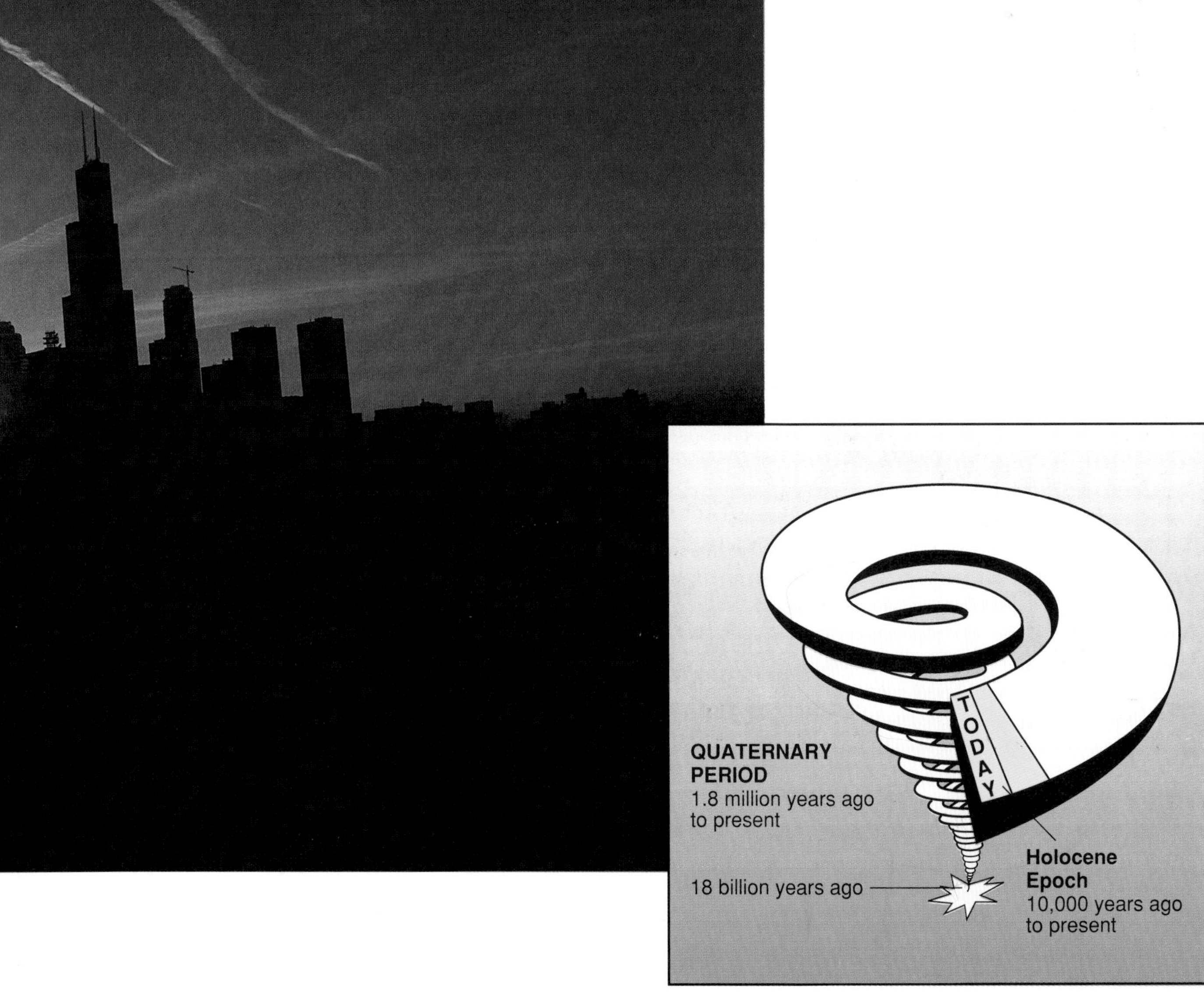

The Holocene Epoch of the Quaternary Period is the name geologists give to the span of time from ten thousand years ago to the present. The climate warmed, and the last of the great ice sheets melted away.

levels rose once more, the land bridge sank beneath the waves and cut off Asia from the Americas. In isolation, the great civilizations of the New World—the Olmec, Maya, Aztec, and Inca—developed independently. The two worlds would meet again, when in the 1500s Spanish explorers claimed the New World for their own.

Technology began when humans deliberately shaped the first stone tools. Humans have mastered the ability to purify and enhance the mineral bounty in Earth's rocks to produce new construction materials. Complex machines can take their creators under the sea and through the air—and even beyond. It is easy to believe that humanity has conquered the planet that spawned it, that Earth is subject to human control.

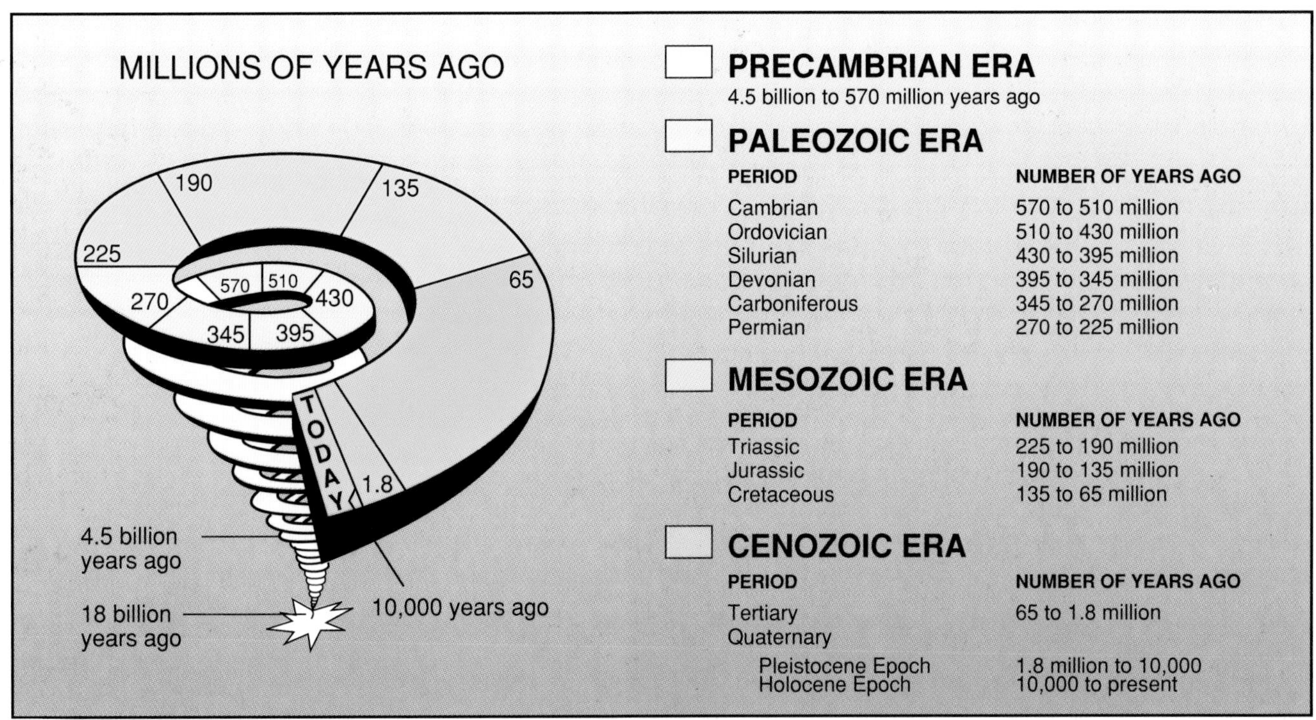

MILLIONS OF YEARS AGO
190
135
225
65
570
510
270
430
345
395
TODAY
1.8
4.5 billion years ago
18 billion years ago
10,000 years ago
PRECAMBRIAN ERA
4.5 billion to 570 million years ago
PALEOZOIC ERA
PERIOD
NUMBER OF YEARS AGO
Cambrian 570 to 510 million
Ordovician 510 to 430 million
Silurian 430 to 395 million
Devonian 395 to 345 million
Carboniferous 345 to 270 million
Permian 270 to 225 million
MESOZOIC ERA
PERIOD
NUMBER OF YEARS AGO
Triassic 225 to 190 million
Jurassic 190 to 135 million
Cretaceous 135 to 65 million
CENOZOIC ERA
PERIOD
NUMBER OF YEARS AGO
Tertiary 65 to 1.8 million
Quaternary
Pleistocene Epoch 1.8 million to 10,000
Holocene Epoch 10,000 to present

This time spiral summarizes the vast span of Earth's history. The entire fossil record so far represents a mere 13 percent of Earth's whole story. And hominids have been walking more or less upright for some three million years—a mere 1/200th of the fossil record. Human civilization is just an eye blink in the history of Earth.

Humanity is far more dependent on Earth than we care to believe. The energy of modern civilization comes largely in the form of oil, coal, and natural gas. These are quite literally fossil fuels, the remains of the great swamps and forests that covered the Earth during Carboniferous times. Fossil fuels are burned to generate electricity, run automobiles, and extract metals from ores. Oil products are also used for lubrication and in the manufacture of dyes, plastics, and drugs.

In the past fifty years, the consumption of fossil fuels has increased dramatically. Whenever oil and coal are burned, carbon dioxide gas is released. Scientists are increasingly concerned that the growing amount of carbon dioxide in Earth's atmosphere will trap more heat from the Sun, beginning a global warming trend that could turn even the richest farmland into desert. Destruction of the world's rain forests may speed the process, since trees consume carbon dioxide in photosynthesis.

A more immediate threat became apparent in the 1980s. Satellites detected a depletion of ozone gas—a hole in the ozone layer—in the atmosphere above Antarctica, as well as less pronounced depletions over the Arctic. Scientists linked this depletion to chemicals used in refrigerators, air conditioners, and spray cans. The ozone layer made it possible for life to venture onto the land, and its loss would again sterilize the Earth's surface.

As we enter 1990s, more and more people are becoming aware of the fragility of the planet Earth. And they are taking action. Yet even as civilization works to understand and correct its mistakes, humans have taken the first bold steps into a hostile new environment—space. What will the future hold for humanity, and for life on Earth?

Only time will tell.

Earth rises over the rugged, lifeless surface of the Moon. Humans have taken the first tentative steps into space and watched the Earth rise over the ancient lunar plains.

Glossary

Age of Reptiles A nickname for the Mesozoic Era, between 225 million and 65 million years ago, when reptiles dominated all the world's environments. It includes the Triassic, Jurassic, and Cretaceous Periods.

Amino acids Any of a group of organic compounds that play a vital role in the chemistry of life. They are the building blocks of proteins.

Ammonite A *cephalopod*—relative of the modern octopus and squid—encased within a flat spiral shell. These arose in the Paleozoic Era, flourished during Mesozoic times, and became extinct at the end of the Cretaceous Period.

Amphibian A moist-skinned animal that lives in both water and air. Adults can breathe air but must return to the water to breed.

Arthropod An invertebrate animal with a jointed body and limbs. Insects, spiders, and lobsters are all arthropods, as were the now-extinct *trilobites.*

Big Bang Nickname for the explosive origin of space, time, and energy—the birth of the universe around us—some eighteen billion years ago.

Blue-green algae A class of simple plants colored by bluish-green pigments. More properly known as *cyanobacteria.*

Brachiopod A marine invertebrate with a clam-like bivalve shell. Brachiopods appeared early in the Paleozoic Era and still survive today.

Cambrian Period A division of geologic time, the first period of the Paleozoic Era. During the Cambrian Period, a wide variety of complex living things evolved but no backboned creatures. *Trilobites* dominated the seas.

Carboniferous Period A period in the Paleozoic Era between 345 and 270 million years ago, named from the vast seams of coal produced from the remains of forests that lived during that time. In Europe it is considered one period, but in North America it is divided into the Mississippian (345 to 310 million years ago) and the Pennsylvanian (310 to 270 million years ago).

Cenozoic Era A major division of geologic time—the Age of Recent Life. It extends from the end of the Mesozoic Era 65 million years ago to the present.

Cephalopod A marine mollusk whose head is surrounded by tentacles, such as the modern squid and octopus. Most fossil cephalopods (*ammonites,* for example) lived within a shell that could be either curved or straight.

Continental drift The term was once used to describe the continuous slow movement of the Earth's continents. It has been replaced by the modern theory of *plate tectonics.*

Cretaceous Period The third and last period of the Mesozoic Era, between 135 and 65 million years ago. Dinosaurs and other reptiles dominated the land, sea, and air but became extinct at the period's close; birds and small mammals also lived.

Crust The outermost layer of a planet or moon.

Devonian Period A period of the Paleozoic Era, between 395 and 345 million years ago. In this period, many kinds of fish were abundant in both fresh and salt water; amphibians evolved from fishes and moved onto the land.

Dinosaur A term meaning "terrible lizard," used to refer to any of a group of extinct carnivorous or herbivorous land-dwelling reptiles that dominated life on Earth during the Mesozoic Era.

DNA Abbreviation for deoxyribonucleic acid, a long, two-stranded molecule coiled like a spiral staircase. It controls the production of amino acids in cells and can make copies of itself. It is the chemical blueprint for life on Earth.

Epoch In geologic time, a subdivision of a period.

Era A major division of geologic time. The Precambrian Era lasted from the Earth's birth to the beginning of the Paleozoic Era—about four billion years. The Paleozoic Era was followed by the Mesozoic and Cenozoic eras. The last three eras are commonly divided into smaller units of time called *periods.*

Fossil The traces or remains of ancient plants or animals—including tracks, burrows, and actual body parts.

Geologic column An idealized sequence of Earth's rocks throughout geologic time.

Geologic time The time extending from the formation of the Earth to the beginning of human history. The part of Earth's history recorded within its rocks.

Globular cluster A dense ball of thousands to millions of stars that orbits around a galaxy.

Half-life The length of time for half the atoms of a *radioactive* substance to decay into different atoms.

Ichthyosaur One of a group of marine reptiles that appeared in the late Triassic Period and survived until the late Cretaceous Period. They reached a length of thirty-three feet (ten meters). Powerful swimmers, they looked similar to modern dolphins.

Invertebrate An animal lacking a spinal column, such a sponge, jellyfish, flatworm, shellfish, octopus, earthworm, insect, spider, and crab.

Jurassic Period A period of the Mesozoic Era, between 190 and 135 million years ago. Dinosaurs were abundant on land at this time, and the first birds appeared.

Mesozoic Era A major division of geologic time—nicknamed the Age of Reptiles. It extends from the end of the Paleozoic Era 225 million years ago to the start of the Cenozoic Era 65 million years ago. It includes the Triassic, Jurassic, and Cretaceous periods.

Meteorite A solid body in orbit around the Sun that strikes the surface of a planet or moon. The impact of one or more giant meteorites probably played a role in the great Cretaceous extinction that killed off the dinosaurs.

Ozone The most chemically active molecule of oxygen, formed by three oxygen atoms.

Ozone layer A region in the Earth's atmosphere about thirty miles (fifty kilometers) up that contains high concentrations of *ozone*. The gas prevents much of the Sun's harmful ultraviolet radiation from reaching Earth's surface.

Paleozoic Era A span of geologic time from 570 to 225 million years ago. It includes the Cambrian, Ordovician, Silurian, Devonian, Carboniferous, and Permian periods.

Period The fundamental unit of geologic time, shorter than an *era* but longer than an *epoch.*

Photosynthesis The process by which green plants manufacture their food using water, carbon dioxide, and the energy in sunlight.

Plate tectonics A theory that explains geologic processes—including volcanoes, earthquakes, and the movement of the continents—as the results of interactions between large, slow-moving plates of Earth's crust.

Precambrian Era All geologic time, and the rocks corresponding to it, before the beginning of the Paleozoic Era about 570 million years ago. It makes up about 90 percent of geologic time.

Quaternary Period A division of the Cenozoic Era, spanning the time from 1.8 million years ago to today. It is divided into two *epochs*: the Pleistocene, which includes the Ice Age, and the Holocene, which runs from about ten thousand years ago to the present.

Radioactivity The spontaneous emission of energy and particles from unstable atoms.

Triassic Period A period of the Mesozoic Era, between 225 and 190 million years ago. Reptiles rose to dominance in the Triassic.

Trilobite An oval-shaped, marine *arthropod* that lived from the Cambrian to the Permian periods. The name refers to the three lobes into which the body is divided.

Vertebrate An animal with a spinal column and backbone. Compare with *invertebrate.*

Index

Numbers in *italics* refer to illustrations or maps.

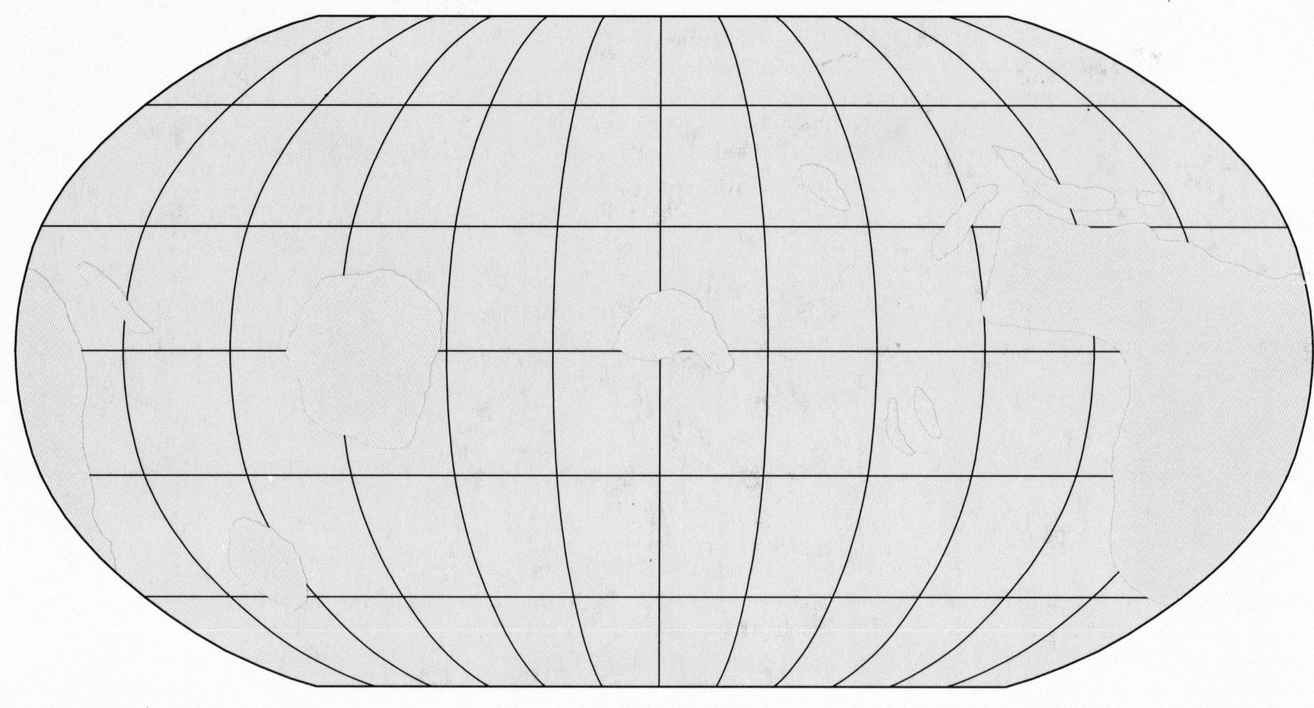

Earth
510 million years ago

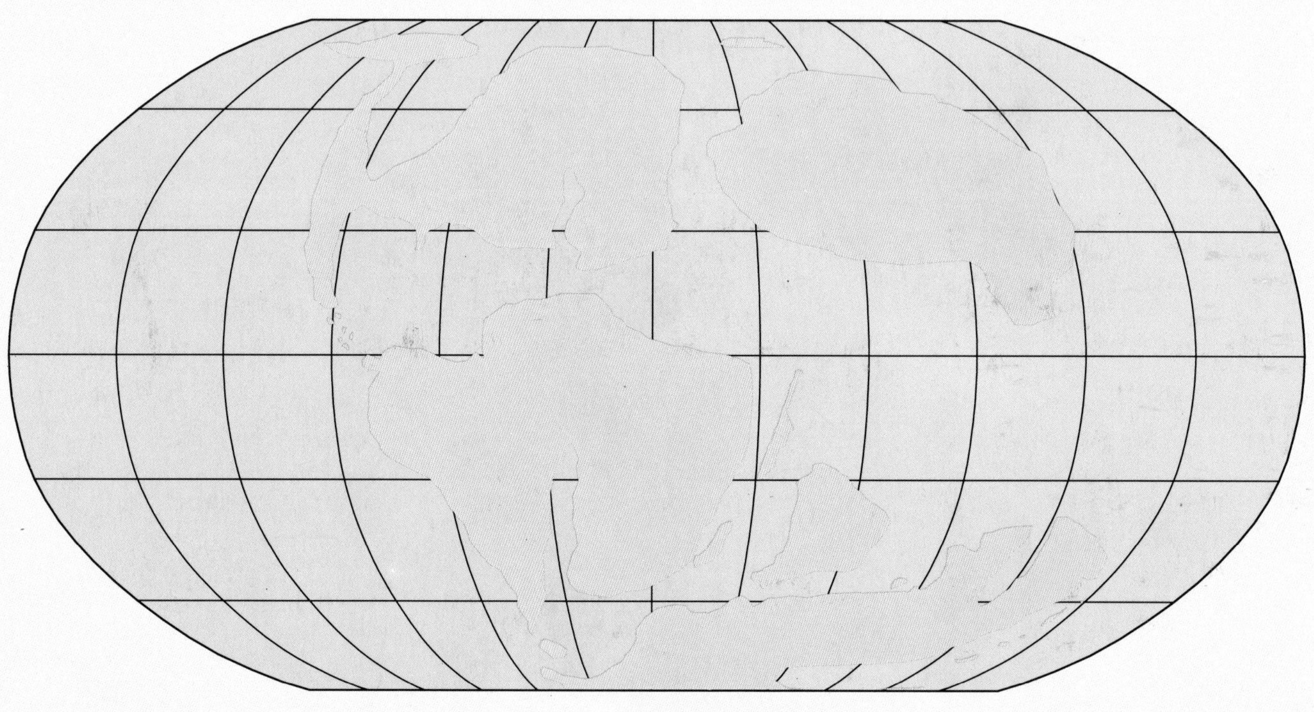

Earth
135 million years ago